National
Geographic
Society

LIVING ON THE

E A R T H

Published by
The National Geographic
Society

Gilbert M. Grosvenor
*President and
Chairman of the Board*

Owen R. Anderson
Executive Vice President

Robert L. Breeden
*Senior Vice President,
Publications and
Educational Media*

Prepared by
National Geographic
Book Service

Charles O. Hyman
Director

Ross S. Bennett
Associate Director

Margaret Sedeen
Managing Editor

Susan C. Eckert
Director of Research

Staff for this book

David F. Robinson
Editor

Leah Bendavid-Val
Illustrations Editor

David M. Seager
Art Director

Paulette L. Claus
Research Editor

Jennifer Gorham Ackerman
Mary B. Dickinson
Edward Lanouette
Carol Bittig Lutyk
Margaret Sedeen
Jonathan B. Tourtellot
Lynn Addison Yorke
Editor-Writers

Marguerite Suarez Dunn
Anne Elizabeth Ely
Catherine Herbert Howell
Joyce B. Marshall
Lise Swinson Sajewski
Penelope A. Timbers
Editorial Researchers

Marguerite Suarez Dunn
Map Coordinator

Lise Swinson Sajewski
Style

Alice Bridget Ching
Kathryn E. Nava
Geography Interns

Marvin W. Mikesell
Professor of Geography,
University of Chicago
Chief Consultant

Charlotte Golin
Design Assistant

David Ross
Illustrations Researcher

Michael Frost
D. Samantha Johnston
Illustrations Assistants

Karen F. Edwards
Traffic Manager

R. Gary Colbert
*Senior Administrative
Assistant*

Teresita Cóquia Sison
Editorial Assistant

George I. Burneston, III
Indexer

John T. Dunn
Technical Director

Richard S. Wain
Production Manager

Andrea Crosman
Production Coordinator

Leslie A. Adams
Production Assistant

David V. Evans
*Quality Control
Manager*

Ratri Banerjee
James B. Enzinna
Werner L. Janney
Anne Meadows
Lise Olney
Melanie Patt-Corner
Robert M. Poole
Shirley L. Scott
Teresita Cóquia Sison
Susan J. Swartz
John Thompson
L. Madison Washburn
Anne E. Withers
Contributors

First edition: 135,000 copies
320 pages, 249 photographs,
plus 9 maps.

Previous page: Centuries-old
terraces transform the slopes
of Bali into level fields, where
rice ripens to feed many people
on land that might otherwise
support only a few.

CONTENTS

EARTH

"Are there many stones in your father's land?" a Berber farmer once asked me in the Rif Mountains of northern Morocco. As we talked, he asked about the amount and timing of rainfall and the hazard of late frost near my home.

To try to explain to him that my father was not a farmer, or that people living near my family home in southern California seldom thought about problems he grappled with daily in the environment of northern Morocco, would have been futile. And a Berber farmer's worries may seem remote and archaic to people living in thriving cities and suburbs. People who take wages and indoor comforts for granted might dismiss "living on the Earth" as an obsolete metaphor. Yet if we learn to understand soil, rainfall, and growing seasons—the conditions that have governed rural life since ancient times—we can understand why some areas are sparsely settled and others are densely settled.

Travelers in western Europe, most of eastern and southern Asia, and the eastern United States rarely lose sight of buildings or cultivated land. But travelers see few signs of civilization between oases in the vast Sahara or between the scattered mining towns, fishing villages, military bases, and other settlements in northern Canada and most of Siberia.

In northern Africa, age-old settlements occupy places that annually receive more than ten inches of rainfall, the minimum needed to grow wheat, barley, and other cereals there. But thin, almost sterile soils inhibit farming in the Amazon basin's sparsely settled tropical rain forest and pre-vent it altogether in the Canadian northlands and Siberia, where the large empty spaces also reflect short growing seasons and—in the tundra zone—poor drainage caused by permanently frozen subsoil.

A population-density map of the world illustrates how environmental advantages and disadvantages affect settlement. The 123,000-square-mile Ganges Plain, one of the most populous areas in the world, has rich soil, abundant water for irrigation, and a year-round growing season. The 850,000-square-mile Tibetan Plateau, thinly settled at best, is high, dry, and windswept. Few valleys offer enough shelter for growing barley or vegetables; most land is used for herding sheep or yaks.

Even more striking is the contrast between the great Saharan void and the intensively cultivated and densely populated Nile Valley. Like most of the Sahara, Egypt is nearly rainless; Cairo receives less than two inches of rainfall annually. Instead, water from the Nile irrigates almost every acre of the country's farmland, making the Nile Valley an enormously long and conspicuous oasis. Groundwater supports plant life at other oases, including Damascus, Syria, which is one of the world's oldest continuously inhabited cities. Although most oases are too small to appear on world maps, oasis dwellers have always been more numerous than pastoral nomads, whose way of life is often thought typical of arid lands.

The largest areas of settlement occur in China and India, where intensive cultivation of rice has sustained dense populations at lower standards of living, and in Europe and the eastern United States, where industry and commerce provide relatively high standards of living. Japan,

Taiwan, and South Korea, where East and West meet in so many ways, support large populations by adopting Western-style industry and commerce, while continuing the Asian tradition of intensively cultivating virtually all arable land.

It is axiomatic that people can live in extreme environments. A temperature of 136°F has been recorded at the Libyan oasis of Azizia, where farmers tend date palms and grow wheat and barley. A temperature of –90°F has been recorded at Verkhoyansk, a small fur-trading post in northeastern Siberia. Inhabitants of the town of Cherrapunji in northeastern India endure 450 inches of annual rainfall, while the copper and nitrate miners and irrigation farmers in the Atacama Desert of Chile may wait decades for a trace of precipitation. Clearly, people who live in remarkable environments find ways to grow a limited amount of food or ways to trade for it. But most people live where the environment permits extensive and reliable food production, or where an abundance of nonagricultural resources or technological advances allow them to import food rather than produce it.

For more than 90 percent of the time humans have lived on Earth, survival depended on hunting and gathering. Moving slowly and without a sense of ultimate destination, small groups of people perpetually searching for game and edible plants reached remote parts of the Earth and perfected skills for surviving in every type of climate and environment.

Looking at a world map or globe, we are awed by the magnitude of this migration. Yet by moving only 20 miles each year, prehistoric trekkers could have covered 2,000 miles—the distance from the Bering Strait to Puget Sound—in a century. Two more centuries could have brought the descendants of Siberian immigrants to the Isthmus of Panama, the gateway to South America. We can only speculate about actual rates of movement, but knowing what was possible gives us hints about how hunters and gatherers managed to spread over the world.

Although more than five billion people now inhabit the Earth, the population probably did not exceed a few million during the millennia that humans spent hunting

and gathering. The fires these humans set to drive game may have encouraged the expansion of grasslands, and hunters may have exterminated the mammoth and a few other species of game. But with ample room and simple Stone Age tools, the hunters and gatherers had relatively little effect on their natural environment compared to the changes farmers would make later. An imaginary astronaut orbiting the Earth in 100,000 B.C. would have seen virgin forests blanketing much of the land, and pristine rivers flowing freely to the seas.

The invention of agriculture about 10,000 years ago initiated a new phase of livelihood. We do not know precisely when or where this most important of innovations took place, but we can trace most of our crops and some of our domesticated animals to a few areas. We believe that people first cultivated barley and wheat in the hilly areas of southwestern Asia; sheep and goats were apparently domesticated there as well. Corn, the great staple of the Americas, probably originated in the highlands of Central America. People in the Andean highlands were the first to domesticate llamas and to grow potatoes. We can trace sweet potatoes back to Mesoamerica, yams to South Asia, and rice to East Asia.

Cultivation of these and other crops spurred the growth of the human family, sometime around 8000 B.C. Henceforth, living on the Earth for most people meant growing crops rather than collecting wild plants, and herding rather than hunting. Populations increased rapidly. People began to enjoy a more secure livelihood. They ceased their endless wandering and began storing their food surpluses and devoting energy to arts, crafts, and other activities. Societies developed specialized groups of warriors, priests, and merchants, as well as artisans and craftsmen. The temporary camps of hunters and gatherers gave way to permanent settlements, which evolved into towns and, eventually, into cities.

As population density increased with the spread of farming and animal husbandry, people modified their environments. Clearing for cultivation meant chopping down trees and exposing soil to erosion. Overgrazing depleted protective plant cov-

7

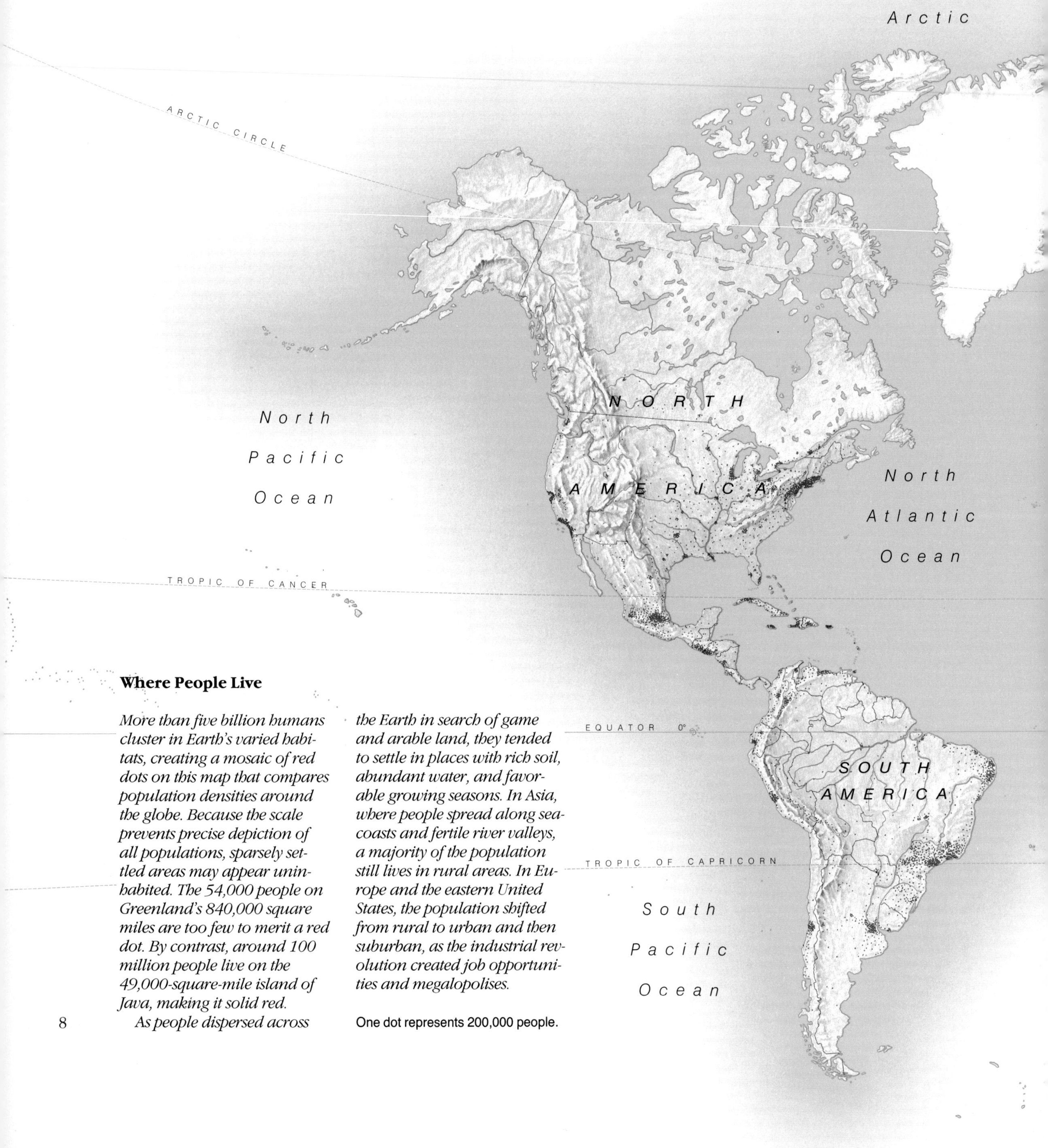

Arctic

ARCTIC CIRCLE

North

Pacific

Ocean

NORTH

AMERICA

North

Atlantic

Ocean

TROPIC OF CANCER

Where People Live

More than five billion humans cluster in Earth's varied habitats, creating a mosaic of red dots on this map that compares population densities around the globe. Because the scale prevents precise depiction of all populations, sparsely settled areas may appear uninhabited. The 54,000 people on Greenland's 840,000 square miles are too few to merit a red dot. By contrast, around 100 million people live on the 49,000-square-mile island of Java, making it solid red.

As people dispersed across

the Earth in search of game and arable land, they tended to settle in places with rich soil, abundant water, and favorable growing seasons. In Asia, where people spread along seacoasts and fertile river valleys, a majority of the population still lives in rural areas. In Europe and the eastern United States, the population shifted from rural to urban and then suburban, as the industrial revolution created job opportunities and megalopolises.

One dot represents 200,000 people.

EQUATOR 0°

SOUTH

AMERICA

TROPIC OF CAPRICORN

South

Pacific

Ocean

Ocean

ASIA

EUROPE

North

Pacific

Ocean

AFRICA

Indian Ocean

AUSTRALIA

South

Atlantic

Ocean

er. Fires set to clear land occasionally raged out of control. And although material comfort improved with the shift from migratory to sedentary life, hygiene deteriorated in crowded settlements, and wastes often contaminated water supplies. An astronaut orbiting the Earth in 1000 B.C. would have seen cultivated fields, forest clearings, villages and cities, irrigation canals, and many other signs of human activity.

Agricultural settlement expanded steadily until well into the age of industrial development, which began in Britain about 200 years ago and eventually provided millions of people with alternatives to rural life. Today, farmers represent less than 3 percent of the U. S. labor force, and service industries employ more than 70 percent of American workers. Population has shifted from rural areas to cities and then to suburbs, not only in countries like Great Britain, Germany, and the United States, which played key roles in early industrial development, but also in countries like Japan, South Korea, and Taiwan, where manufacturing and trade are relatively new and explosive developments. In the world's developing countries, roughly a third of the populace lives in cities.

Industrialization and urbanization introduced a new phase of environmental change. Air and water pollution, waste-disposal problems, and the combination of suburban sprawl and inner-city blight pose familiar dilemmas. Immense settlements of squatters ring many of the cities of Latin America and Asia. Yet the influx of job seekers continues as more and more people see earning a paycheck, rather than producing food, as the best or only way to live.

Living on the Earth is a grand theme, encompassing all of human experience and offering opportunities to appreciate how particular people live in specific places. Humans share a common heritage of trials and errors and a pattern of land use exhibiting both success and failure. Ironically, although the Inuit of the Arctic and the Mbuti of Africa's Ituri Forest display exceptional levels of ingenious adaptation to their environment, change is encroaching on their habitats and undermining their traditions. The Berber farmer might merit high marks for tenacity and skill in scratching out a living on the rocky slopes in northern Morocco, but his land is too steep for long-term farming without terracing, and the gullies that eventually dissect his fields reveal his ultimate failure to cope with serious problems of erosion.

Each of Earth's habitats presents special opportunities and special problems. For example, the richest of all agricultural habitats is found on the floodplains of rivers such as the Nile, Tigris-Euphrates, and Indus. There, fertile soil, abundant water, and long growing seasons provide seemingly ideal conditions for producing food, and dense populations offer emphatic evidence of sustained productivity. Moreover, each of these valleys cradled an ancient civilization. But people living near all of these rivers have endured destructive flooding, choked irrigation channels, and silted reservoirs. In areas like the Tigris-Euphrates and Indus Valleys, where rates of evaporation are high, heavy irrigation can contaminate the soil with salts and leave cement-like crusts on once productive land.

The North American prairie also rates as an exceptionally rich habitat. Today this natural grassland is one of the world's breadbaskets, but when pioneer farmers first encountered the prairie, they were skeptical of the treeless land, which they considered an odd form of desert. Although they later realized that rainfall was sufficient to produce spectacular harvests, plowing the thick prairie sod remained a formidable task until the invention of a self-scouring steel plow in the 1830s. Prairie farmers also contended with vast fires that struck the grasslands during summer thunderstorm seasons in the 19th century. Erosion and droughts turned the drier western margin of the prairie into a dust bowl in the 1930s. Today, because of agriculture, tall-grass prairie as natural vegetation is nearly extinct in North America as well as in Argentina, Hungary, and the Soviet Union.

The harsh arctic and desert environments have posed the greatest challenges for humans. Seizing every opportunity in

10

their chilly habitat, the Inuit learned to build snug shelters of snow; other northern people of Canada, Greenland, Alaska, and Siberia used sod or hides. People made their clothing from the skins of animals—perfect natural protection against the harsh weather. The Inuit developed an array of hunting skills adapted to various conditions and available resources. They hunted on ice during the long arctic winter, and from kayaks during periods of thaw; some pursued caribou overland during the short summer season. But traditional Inuit culture has declined as technology has offered new opportunities for a modern life-style. Today, motorboats and snowmobiles have replaced kayaks and dogsleds in the hunt for food. And the Alaskan oil industry now provides jobs and revenue that were unavailable in the past.

The Bedouin tribes in countries like Saudi Arabia, Syria, Jordan, and Iraq learned to survive the rigors of desert life by migrating with the seasons to get water or to find suitable places to graze their camels, sheep, or goats. The Bedouin traditionally served as caravan guardians and guides and collected tribute from oasis villages, which these nomads protected from raiders. Today, the villagers continue to trade manufactured goods for meat, wool, and milk products of the Bedouin herds. But the 20th century has seen the Bedouin way of life fade, as new political boundaries drawn across the lands of the former Ottoman Empire in North Africa and southwestern Asia after World War I cut across the nomads' grazing lands. Some Bedouin have become farmers, while others have taken jobs with oil companies. Many have bought trucks and now earn their living hauling or trading goods. But a few have kept their camels, looking ahead to the day when oil no longer flows in the desert.

Deforestation is an ancient form of environmental modification: People had to clear land before they could cultivate it. In many parts of the world, this process has advanced so much that forests exist only in regions where few humans live. When farmland replaces forests in relatively small areas, the principal harm is likely to be aesthetic. But when trees are removed from steep slopes, erosion may destroy the land. Erosion caused by deforestation has driven farmers from their land in highland areas of the Middle East and has caused catastrophic destruction in the Himalayan foothills.

When forests consist of just a few types of trees, as in Canada, destruction does not entail a genetic loss. But deforestation is a much more serious problem in a tropical rain forest, where thousands of plant and animal species may occur in a single acre. Damage to this kind of ecosystem is irreversible. The massive clearing of tropical rain forest, especially in Brazil, has resulted in the loss of a significant part of the Earth's genetic diversity. In lands ranging from Panama to Borneo, native populations face the chain saws and bulldozers of progress. At the urging of alarmed geneticists and ecologists, UNESCO has established biosphere reserves in the forests of dozens of nations around the world.

It is easy to associate vanishing cultures and endangered species with a more familiar litany of modern woes including air and water pollution, ozone depletion, and toxic waste. Perhaps these problems seem remote to people who associate the outdoors with recreation rather than livelihood or limit their encounters with the environment to dashing between air-conditioned automobiles and air-conditioned offices and homes. But we need to remember that we share the experience of living on the Earth with all of the world's people through all of human time. It is said that we do not inherit the land from our parents, we borrow it from our children.

The distinctive challenge of our time is that there is no remaining land where we can escape the consequences of our growing population or the mismanagement of our environment. In many places, as in the U. S., we reached the last great frontiers of settlement in the 19th century; vast stretches of virgin land waiting for pioneers no longer exist. The tenacity and ingenuity evident during the millennia of human expansion over the Earth must now be directed to an urgent problem: How can we manage our limited resources to sustain a good—or at least tolerable—life for an ever increasing human population?

MARVIN W. MIKESELL

LIVING IN
ARID LANDS

"I tell you," said Sheikh Mohamed Al-Rashed as he sat in his comfortably appointed living room on the outskirts of Kuwait City, "today's generation has lost touch with the land." The 92-year-old patriarch had been regaling family and friends with tales of desert life in days gone by—long before the discovery of vast oil deposits transformed this once somnolent fishing, pearling, and trading village on the Persian Gulf into a 20th-century high-rise metropolis of steel and concrete and glass.

"My own sons," he said, gesturing to a handsome group of Western-educated professionals, "would be lost in the desert just a few kilometers from where we live."

"Weren't you ever lost in the desert?" teased one of the sons.

"Never," asserted the old sheikh. "Even in the worst of dust or sandstorms my companions and I could find our way without a compass, and bow in the direction of Mecca for our prayers.

"How?" he went on. "We felt the stones on the ground. Their pitted surface always faced northwest, because this is the direction from which the *shamal* wind blows."

As I listened to this extraordinary man, I noticed that his attire did not differ markedly from that of his sons. All wore the full-length robe called a *dishdasha,* and the *ghutra,* a white head covering.

But what a difference between the life experiences of these two generations. As a child, the sheikh had lived in a mud-brick house, sleeping and playing on sheep's-wool rugs. His children, by contrast, had grown to adulthood in a spacious villa furnished with beds and sofas—and with conveniences such as plumbing and electricity, air-conditioning and television.

The town of his youth is unrecognizable now. Oil revenues have fueled its growth into a sprawling city, with scarcely a pitted stone left to point direction. The sheikh and his traveling companions had bowed toward Mecca in prayer five times a day; his sons, because of the demands of modern life, barely find time to pray once or twice a day. Sheikh Al-Rashed has lived through many changes, some of them drastic. Now he feels uneasy, fearful that the desert life he had known is vanishing like water cast on burning sand.

Throughout the world, arid-land cultures have evolved in different ways. But all have responded to the same environmental constraint: dryness. By one traditional measure, any place that receives less than ten inches of rain a year can be defined as a desert. But precipitation alone does not tell the tale. Evaporation, too, plays an important part, as do other factors such as soil and vegetation. In parts of the Sahara, Peruvian, and Atacama deserts, solar and ground radiation can evaporate up to 200 times the moisture received, making these deserts the world's driest.

Atmospheric conditions produce most of the large deserts—the Sahara, the deserts of central and western Australia, and the arid arc that sweeps from northwestern India and southern Pakistan through Afghanistan, Iran, Iraq, and the Arabian Peninsula. These arid lands coincide with twin high-pressure areas of dry air that encircle the globe roughly along the Tropics of Cancer and Capricorn.

Other deserts exist because of their remoteness from the oceans with their moisture-laden air masses. Such is the case with the Turkestan Desert and the Gobi of central Asia. Still others, including the Patagonian Desert of South America, are formed in places where mountains intercept moisture-carrying winds, creating arid rain shadows on their leeward sides.

Cold ocean currents, too, by cooling the air above them, keep rain clouds from forming, a temperature-inversion condition largely responsible for South America's Atacama Desert and the Namib Desert along the coast of southwestern Africa.

Deserts make up about a fifth of Earth's landmass. Include the semiarid lands that often border them, areas such as the Great Basin of North America and the arid regions around the Caspian Sea in Europe, and the proportion increases to a third. These semideserts, mostly scrublands and seasonal grasslands, blend almost imperceptibly into true deserts. If irrigated or blessed with adequate rain, some semideserts can support farm crops and lush pasturage. But when the rains fail, as they have

Water, more precious than diamonds in a dusty land, slakes the thirst of a boy on Aboriginal land in Australia's Gibson Desert. Behind him, a windmill's skeletal shadow falls across a landscape that gets less than ten inches of rainfall a year.

Today, nearly a billion people inhabit the world's arid lands. More than 100 nations face the threat of expanding deserts—for which man and nature often share the blame.

PREVIOUS PAGE: A Tuareg craftsman in Niger fire-hardens a soapstone arm ring thought to bring luck to its wearer.

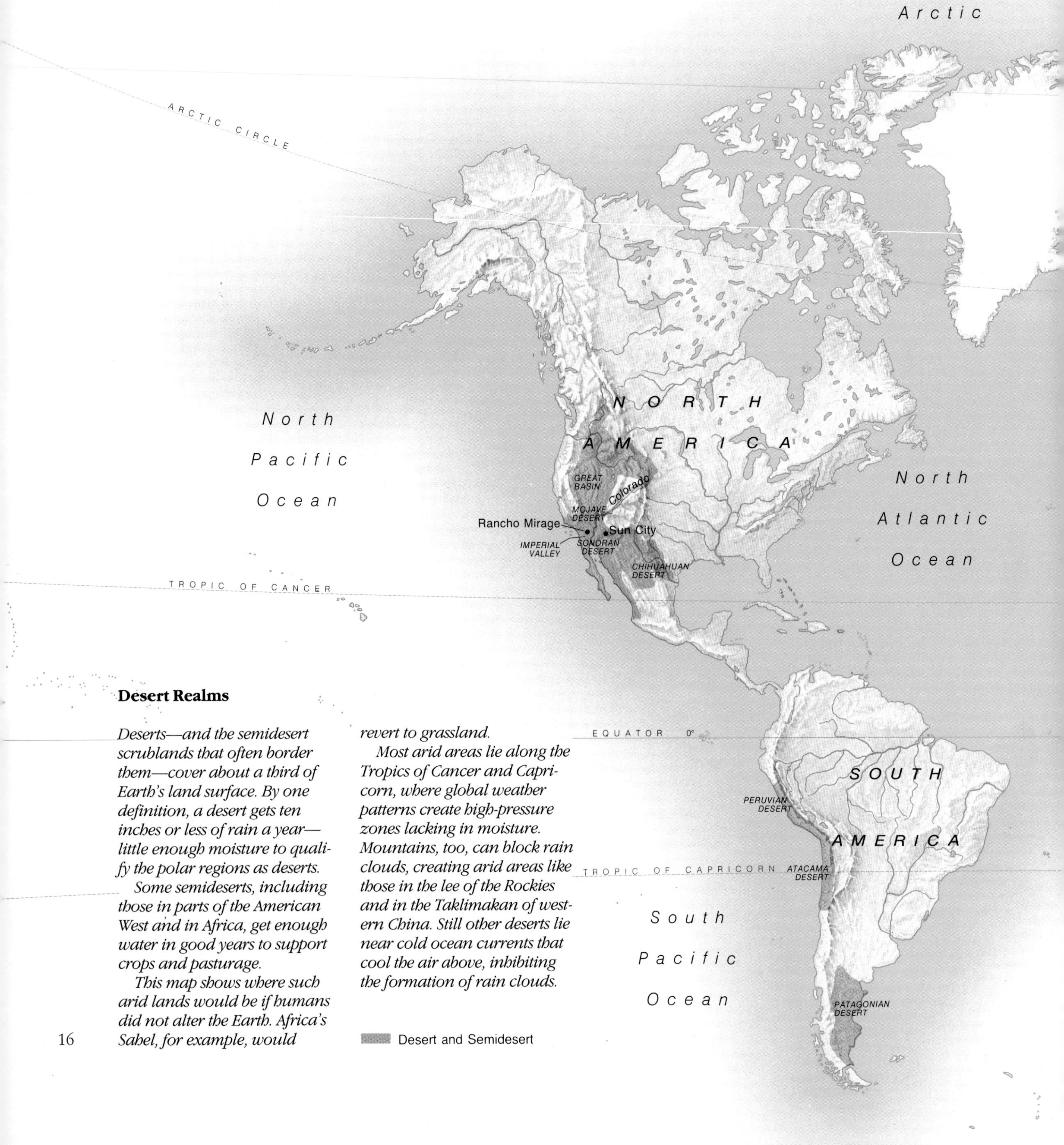

Arctic

ARCTIC CIRCLE

North

Pacific

Ocean

NORTH

AMERICA

GREAT
BASIN

Colorado

MOJAVE
DESERT

Rancho Mirage • •Sun City

IMPERIAL
VALLEY

SONORAN
DESERT

CHIHUAHUAN
DESERT

North

Atlantic

Ocean

TROPIC OF CANCER

Desert Realms

Deserts—and the semidesert
scrublands that often border
them—cover about a third of
Earth's land surface. By one
definition, a desert gets ten
inches or less of rain a year—
little enough moisture to quali-
fy the polar regions as deserts.

Some semideserts, including
those in parts of the American
West and in Africa, get enough
water in good years to support
crops and pasturage.

This map shows where such
arid lands would be if humans
did not alter the Earth. Africa's
Sahel, for example, would

revert to grassland.

Most arid areas lie along the
Tropics of Cancer and Capricorn, where global weather
patterns create high-pressure
zones lacking in moisture.
Mountains, too, can block rain
clouds, creating arid areas like
those in the lee of the Rockies
and in the Taklimakan of western China. Still other deserts lie
near cold ocean currents that
cool the air above, inhibiting
the formation of rain clouds.

EQUATOR   0°

SOUTH

AMERICA

PERUVIAN
DESERT

TROPIC OF CAPRICORN   ATACAMA
DESERT

South

Pacific

Ocean

PATAGONIAN
DESERT

16

■ Desert and Semidesert

Ocean

North

Pacific

Ocean

ASIA

EUROPE

Turpan
Oasis

GOBI

TURKESTAN
DESERT

TAKLIMAKAN
DESERT

TENGGER
DESERT

DASHT-E KAVIR

DASHT-E LUT

NEGEV

SYRIAN
DESERT

SAHARA

Faiyum
Oasis

WESTERN
DESERT

LIBYAN DESERT

Beersheba

Kuwait

GREAT
INDIAN
DESERT
RAJASTHAN

TÉNÉRÉ
DESERT

SINAI

Riyadh

ARABIAN
DESERT

Nouakchott

Aswan

Kharga
Oasis

RUB AL KHALI

Timbuktu

Gao

Nile

S   SAHEL

AFRICA

Tug
Wajale

Somali
Peninsula

CHALBI
DESERT

Indian Ocean

AUSTRALIA

GREAT
SANDY DESERT

SIMPSON
DESERT

GIBSON DESERT

NAMIB
DESERT

KALAHARI
DESERT

GREAT VICTORIA
DESERT

STURT
STONY
DESERT

South

Atlantic

Ocean

in the Sahel region bordering the Sahara, famine and disease can wreak havoc.

The word "desert" evokes specific images in our minds, many of them misconceptions. Most deserts, for example, are not covered by shifting sand dunes. Even the Sahara is only 20 percent sand. The rest is solid rock and *hammada,* rock covered with pebbles. Nearly the entire Sturt Stony Desert of Australia is strewn with loose pebbles and stones. The hammada-like *gobi* plains of central Asia, which make up 44 percent of China's desert landscape, give their name to the better known desert.

Nor are deserts invariably hot and dry. Altitude and latitude make the deserts of central Asia and South America cold much of the year. Even in the Sahara daily temperatures can fluctuate 100°F or more—enough to freeze the unprotected traveler to death. And when rain does fall in the desert, its effects can be devastating. In California's Death Valley, the driest spot in North America, more people drown in flash floods than die of thirst.

As might be expected, the life-styles of desert inhabitants vary widely, depending on terrain, climate, and state of economic development. Arid-land dwellers can be traders, herders, farmers—even city dwellers in places such as Tucson, Arizona, or Riyadh, Saudi Arabia.

As a youngster born and raised in Egypt —itself 96 percent desert—I have long been fascinated by the incredible variety of deserts and their inhabitants. My interest, and later my training as a geologist, led me to travel in dry lands all over the world to better understand how deserts originate and how they evolve through cycles of expansion and contraction.

My introduction to the desert came while on youthful scouting trips to the Muqattam and El Ahmar mountains east of Cairo. In these bare rock mountains, the colorful sandstones, weird shapes, and mysterious caves bade me visit again and again.

One trip, the 50-mile journey by bus from Cairo to the Faiyum Oasis, made an especially lasting impression. The road was not paved in those days and our bus bounced over hard rock for hours. Then it ran into a field (Continued on page 25)

Servants draw water for the thirsty herds of a Tuareg chief in Niger. The chief ultimately lost thousands of cattle as a drought that began in 1968 brought famine and devastation to the Sahel, a broad seasonal grassland reaching across sub-Saharan Africa. Modern wells encouraged nomadic pastoralists to set up permanent encampments, where their livestock soon overgrazed the fragile land. Farmers cut trees for firewood and, encouraged by the government, planted soil-depleting cash crops such as peanuts and cotton. As the drought continued into the 1970s and '80s, many once proud nomads were forced to seek jobs in overcrowded cities or languish in refugee camps.

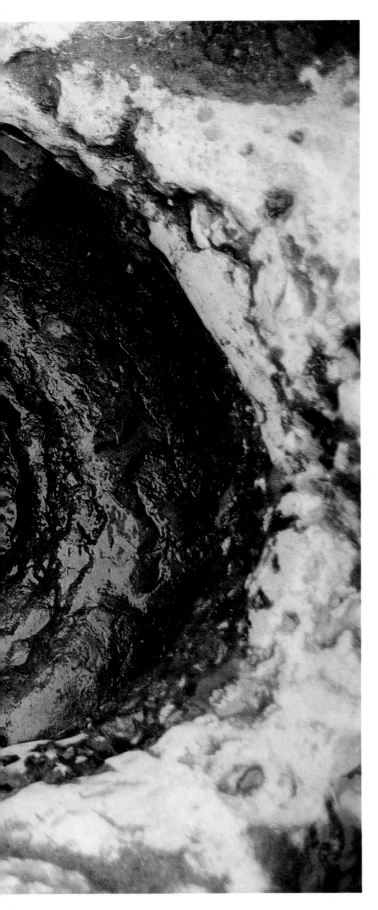

Fetching the water often falls to women and children in desert families. A Somali youth (left) scoops water from a hole fed by an underground river. In Niger, Wodaabe women (above) haul water from a well in a goatskin bag.

NEXT PAGE: *A Tuareg salt caravan, navigating by sun and stars, sways across the Ténéré Desert in Niger. Able to carry a quarter-ton load, a camel has broad, padded feet that allow it to negotiate soft sands that would stop a truck.*

21

of sand and lurched to a halt. We all climbed out and helped to pull it free, an exercise repeated a few miles farther on.

At last we crested a rise and, suddenly, the land sloped downward into a brilliant green swath, a lush oasis that spread as far as the eye could see—far bigger than the popular perception of an oasis as a place with a few palm trees and a camel. Here stood many villages, in addition to Faiyum itself, then a city of 100,000 people. An oasis, whether large or small, natural or manmade, is an area made verdant by water in an otherwise arid expanse.

As we drove deeper into the Faiyum, the temperature dropped appreciably; the shade of fig trees beckoned us to picnic. In the fields of cotton and rice around us, farmers sang as they brought up water from canals. Women worked in their mud huts and built cooking fires, or tended flocks of sheep. Children ran behind donkeys laden with hay, prodding them to move faster.

At that time, I had not realized that the whole Faiyum Oasis was a desert-reclamation project from ancient days, fields made fertile by Nile water channeled into canals originally dug nearly 3,800 years ago, during the reign of Amenemhet III.

What I saw in the Faiyum resembled the familiar village scenes in the heart of the Nile Delta, with its many fields and numerous communities. Thus, 750 miles of the Nile's course through Egypt may be considered an oasis in the vast and arid reaches of the eastern Sahara.

Throughout the world, dry environments have shaped the way people dress, eat, build, behave, and think. Perhaps nothing has affected the clothing of desert dwellers more than sun and heat. In the arid lands of Australia and southern Africa, where the sun is not quite as strong, the natives customarily wore little or no clothing. But in the searing heat of the great sand deserts almost all people, whether the Tuareg of North Africa, Tibbu of the Tibesti Mountains northeast of Lake Chad, or Bedouin of Arabia, wear a loose, robe-like garment. It is also common for them to wear a headdress such as the turban and veil of the Tuareg, and the *kufieya* or ghutra of the Bedouin.

Such attire limits loss of body water and reduces thirst, a factor overlooked by desert troops from Western nations, whose clothing is more appropriate to milder, wetter climates. Their uniforms—shirts and belted shorts with knee socks, or fatigues—constrict air movement over the body, leaving the men to swelter. Their berets expose their necks and faces to blistering sun and blowing sand. Even when the robe and headdress was part of tradition, as in Egypt, the late President Nasser asked his people to adopt Western-style clothing in the name of modernization.

Water—or its lack—has shaped the habits and patterns of life in dry lands. Bedouin learn to drink water sparingly, sometimes only once a day. They take every chance to save water, even during religious rituals. Normally, Muslims wash their faces, hands, and feet before facing God in prayer. But in the desert they use dry, clean sand to perform this ablution.

The scarcity of water has engendered nomadism, a way of life given to wandering in search of water and the vegetation it creates. Thus nomads have developed a keen awareness of rainfall patterns and move in small groups to avoid overtaxing limited resources. Both the Aborigines of Australia's outback and the San (Bushmen) of the Kalahari have such an acute knowledge of their environment that they know where and when to move to exploit seasonal rainfall and the edible plants it nurtures.

Because of their sensitivity to preserving the range, pastoral nomads know when to break camp to prevent their animals from overgrazing, for they know that they will return to the old range. Such knowledge comes from thousands of years of living in a place where the only constant is the scarcity of resources. In Arabia, it is said that the longest tribal war, a 40-year feud that took place some 1,500 years ago, began when a camel belonging to one tribe was allowed to graze in an area deemed off limits for the season by another tribe.

In the deserts of Africa and Asia, oases play a crucial role in the lives of nomads. Many oases are about a week's camel march

In a land of searing heat and meager shadows, Tuareg nomads of Niger's southern Sahara region create their own shade with tents. Over a wooden frame, a family stretches a roof of goatskins tanned and dyed with clay. In the past, important chiefs lived in tents made of 60 or 70 skins. Today many Tuareg shelters are roofed with cloth. The open-walled dwelling admits cooling breezes. During storms, woven grass mats erected as walls offer protection from blowing sand. The Tuareg sweep their sandy floors daily and spread carpets for visitors. Families regularly dismantle their tents and load belongings on camels or trucks to journey to more promising pastures.

25

Somali nomads, like many other people of the desert, find portable homes ideal for their wandering way of life. After lashing branches together in a conical framework, women attach woven mats of palm fiber or of grass and bark. A bride's dowry includes materials and furnishings for an aqal, as the hut is known, and she takes charge of building and moving it during the marriage. But the aqal goes to her husband if he divorces her for barrenness or adultery.

Outside a completed hut, mother and child relax behind a fence of thornbushes that protects the settlement from hyenas, jackals, and other marauders, and serves as a corral for sheep and goats.

26

apart—a day's drive by car. A camel can go a week or so without a drink during the heat of summer, losing up to a third of its weight without lasting ill effect.

To watch a camel drink water after a week on the march is a memorable experience. Water does not stay long in the camel's stomach, as was once commonly believed. Instead it enters into the cells that form the animal's muscles and other tissues. You can almost see the camel swell up before your eyes as it gulps water in enormous quantities—30 gallons or more—to quench a desert thirst.

The Bedouin say that if you sing to your camel, it will serve you better. Many times I have ridden in a car with a Bedouin driver when he would suddenly launch into a loud, wailing song. The singing didn't make the car run better, but it certainly broke the boredom and monotony of the ride.

Most nomads are passionate in their love of life in the open desert. To them, cities are anathema—confining, crowded, dirty, noisy, oppressive. In the boundless expanses of the desert they have freedom to roam and to express themselves, a freedom particularly noticeable in the dress and behavior of the women. In the Muslim cities of Africa and parts of Asia, women often dress in black, wear veils, and lead sequestered lives. But in the deserts of these lands women frequently wear very colorful dresses and enjoy greater freedom of movement. Nomad women, unlike their city-dwelling sisters, are much less sheltered and hidden away. They tend to the herds and exercise more control over household affairs. Arabian Bedouin women even have learned to drive cars and trucks, something unheard of in the cities.

Many nomads are traders. Some Tuareg, for instance, spend much of their lives transporting salt to and from towns across the Sahara. Others, such as the Wodaabe of central Niger, are herders. For thousands of

Mud—cheap, plentiful, and practical wherever timber is scarce—long has served as a building material in arid areas. Today about half the world's people live in houses made of adobe—mud mixed with straw or grass. To make their earthen bricks, Somali women (right) knead mud to a proper consistency. An Egyptian mason (above) shapes his bricks in a wooden mold and then sun dries or bakes them in a kiln. In Saudi Arabia (opposite) a worker lays out a grid of unbaked brick to dry.

28

Villagers in Mauritania toss dusty waves back into the sea of sand that daily laps against their schoolhouse. Dunes have engulfed many settlements, forcing residents to abandon their homes to the sand.

Climate changes make deserts grow or shrink periodically, but the inhabitants of Africa's arid Sahel region have hastened desert expansion in recent years by cutting trees and shrubs, planting inappropriate crops, and overgrazing the land. Now, stripped of stabilizing plant life, the Sahel succumbs to the desert at a rate of about 12 million acres a year.

years their culture has been based almost entirely on cattle. And in the arid reaches of Australia's outback, a few Aborigines still lead nomadic lives as hunters and gatherers, sustaining themselves on whatever plants and animals they can forage.

The availability of water in the desert varies considerably from place to place. I once accompanied the field director of Egypt's Geological Survey during a visit to the deserts of Arizona. After several stops to view terrain covered with mesquite, greasewood, yucca, and various cactus species, he asked, "When do we get to the desert?"

"This *is* the desert," I replied.

"How lucky are the Americans," he murmured. "Even their desert is a jungle!"

I knew what he meant. For eyes accustomed to the empty stretches of North Africa and Arabia, the deserts of North America seem almost gardenlike. In truth most are semideserts, at times and places receiving more than 20 inches of moisture a year—ten times more than the Sahara. Time and again I have driven across great expanses of Egypt's Western Desert without seeing as much as a blade of grass.

Lack of vegetation also means a lack of large wild animals, making most deserts extraordinarily quiet places. The profound silence can unnerve people accustomed to the ordinary sounds of town and country, and takes time to get used to.

But deserts are not always quiet. Winds blowing across the great empty reaches can moan and groan eerily. Then there are the mysterious "singing sands." Marco Polo in the 13th century wrote of dunes in the Taklimakan Desert that gave off sounds like "the strains of many instruments." More recently, a Chinese colleague told me that, while he was sliding down a dune near Dunhuang, the sand began to bellow like a herd of cattle. And I myself, while in the Sinai, once heard sounds resembling the muffled shrieks of a soprano voice.

Sands that howl, shriek, and roar where no living thing exists: Is it any wonder that Arab Bedouin attribute such phenomena to djinn, capricious spirits, and that they try

31

to avoid singing-dune areas at all costs?

No one knows how the sounds are produced. My own theory is that dry sand grains become electrically charged when they slide downslope. The noise, if this theory is correct, comes from the discharges of millions of these sliding particles.

Travel in arid lands leaves a lasting impression of the dominance of wind as an agent of erosion, transport, and deposition of dust and sand. Wind also probably helped determine the shape of many desert dwellers' houses. Throughout arid environments—and other windy places too—people often build round or dome-shaped houses, perhaps because such dwellings can withstand buffeting winds better than square or rectangular structures.

I was reminded of this when I visited a yurt on the windy plains near the Gobi of Mongolia. A circular structure, the yurt can withstand winds of up to 90 miles an hour. Its framework is made of willow or poplar withes lashed together to form a circular, lattice-like wall surmounted by a dome- or cone-shaped roof. The framework is covered by felt and hides to protect the inhabitants from the cold wind. In the Great Indian Desert of northwestern India similar structures made of wood, straw, and mud are used to store grain.

In contrast to the austere world outside, the interior of the yurt I visited blazed with color. On the bright red carpet my host arranged dried goat's-milk cheese. He insisted I have some with the tea, which his wife served in tall porcelain mugs.

Mud brick—or adobe, from the Arabic *at tuba*—is used as a building material throughout arid lands from Afghanistan and the mountains of Yemen to the canyons of the American Southwest. Pueblo Indians build with adobe to this day; their predecessors, the cliff-dwelling Anasazi, used mud to plaster their stone dwellings.

The brick is made by mixing soil, water, and chopped straw, in some cases with dung or sand. Baked in the sun, mud bricks are cheap and easy to make. Mud is also a poor conductor of heat, and keeps the temperature of houses up to 30 degrees cooler inside than outside, a fact often overlooked in the rush to modernize.

Hunger often stalks the Sahel, where from 1968 to 1973 drought brought on famine and disease that killed 250,000 people and millions of animals. In Burkina Faso, women of the Bella tribe (opposite) probe a crusted riverbed for potato-like roots of water lilies that once bloomed here. Milk sustains many nomads. Somali herders (right, upper) milk their camels twice a day. Even when they drink brackish water, camels give sweet milk.

Mother's milk nourishes a Somali child (right, lower). Where food and water are scarce, children may nurse until four years old. This increases the chances for the youngsters' survival and limits birthrates by delaying pregnancies.

A woman in the dry northwestern state of Rajasthan in India (right) shapes cow-dung disks to dry in the sun for use as fuel. People who live in treeless areas often burn dried dung for cooking and heating. But by doing so, they deprive thin soils of badly needed fertilizer, heightening food shortages as crop yields shrink and population grows.

Rajasthani women (above) use their heads to transport heaping baskets of the sun-cured patties, enough to last about a week.

34

"Go see the ghost towns the government built for us," said Saleh Abdo, a 30-year-old Nubian whose family and fellow villagers had been uprooted and relocated to escape the rising Nile water when the Aswan High Dam was built in the 1960s. He referred to the modern cement-block villages the Egyptian government had built to replace the domed mud-brick clusters traditionally built by Nubians living along the Nile.

"We call them the cement graves," he lamented, "and for years my father lived outdoors rather than suffocate in those abominable furnaces."

I had felt the great drop in temperature when I walked into mud-brick houses in the new village of Baris in the Kharga Oasis. The village had been built as a model by maverick Egyptian architect Hassan Fathy, now in his 80s. But his ideas had been scorned by government planners bent on "modernization" and the village never became a viable community.

By studying the past, Fathy has found a key to the future. His structures fit the environment, using ancient techniques and inexpensive, readily available resources— human beings, soil and sand, a little water, straw, and the drying power of the sun.

In recent years Fathy designed and built an Islamic center near Santa Fe, New Mexico, using mud-brick walls and Nubian vault-and-dome technology to help keep the buildings cool. His ideas have also been used in Arabia and in other parts of Africa. Thus the Nubian arches and domes may someday regain their rightful place among modern arid-land housing designs.

As it is with constructing a house, so it is with surviving from day to day in the desert: Both require ingenuity. The San, or Bushmen, for example, have devised a unique system of "sip wells" for tapping water from the sands of the Kalahari. First they locate an area where water lies close to the surface, usually a place where the water has been trapped below ground by an impermeable layer of hardened soil. They then dig down to the water, pack grass into the hole, and insert a hollow reed into

Biscuits from a bouldery oven: Like many desert cooks, this Somali baker (opposite) lacks a steady supply of local ingredients and so must use imported grain. Poor soils and sparse rainfall limit the crops farmers can grow without irrigation, and larders empty quickly in drought years.

Chaff and grain cascade from one calabash to another as a Wodaabe woman winnows millet. She will pound the grain with a heavy pestle for several hours, then boil the flour with water and add vegetables or milk to make gruel. These nomadic herders do not normally raise crops, but sell precious livestock to buy millet that supplements their skimpy dry-season diet.

the grass. The hole is mounded over with sand and air is sucked out through the reed, creating a vacuum that draws water into the hole. The collected water is then sipped through the reed.

Such wells provide only part of the San's daily water needs. Central Kalahari bands must seek up to 90 percent of their water and nourishment from large bulbs and wild melons such as the tsama and gemsbok varieties that can weigh more than 100 pounds and hold several gallons of liquid.

In central Australia, roaming bands of Aborigines were renowned for their ability to find water in unlikely places. The roots of certain trees, including a desert oak, provided a refreshing drink. So did the liquid-filled membrane in which a desert-dwelling frog encased itself below ground in the dry seasons. To get a drink, the Aborigine stamped the ground, listening for a telltale croak, then dug up the frog with a stick and wrung the water from the sac.

Both the San and the Aborigines also relied on bushes and occasional trees to provide them with building materials, tools and weapons, and musical instruments. Today the way of life of both groups is disappearing as their ancestral ties with the land give way to resettlement, paying jobs, and modern conveniences.

In the American Southwest, the Hopi Indians of northeastern Arizona live in a scattering of centuries-old villages located on the tops of mesas. They long ago mastered the techniques of dry farming, planting their corn, melons, beans, and squash in depressions and along dry streambeds where moisture and runoff from infrequent rains accumulate. To protect the young plants from blowing sand they erected simple windbreaks of rocks or brush or, more recently, of empty cans with the bottoms knocked out.

Their neighbors the Navajos, whose lands today surround the Hopi, have adapted to their arid world by changing lifestyles as they migrated southward from the forests of Canada about 500 years ago. Once hunters of deer and elk and gatherers of wild vegetables in Canada, the Navajos

settled down and learned farming from the Hopi. Under Spanish influence in the 19th century, they also took up horse raising, and herding sheep, cattle, and goats.

Shifting dunes and sand deposits menace desert dwellers around the world, whether they live in a Tuareg oasis in Algeria, a mining town in the Namib, or a cattle station in Australia's outback.

In North Africa the traditional response to sand encroachment has been to plant a line of trees to barricade the approaching sand. The tactic slows the sand, but rarely stops it. In India, scientists from the Central Arid Zone Research Institute in Rajasthan have erected parallel fences of hay on top of gently rolling dunes. Their efforts, too, have been largely unavailing.

But in the Tengger Desert of western China, desert researchers may have found a solution to the problem of wandering dunes: They anchor them with a gridlike network of straw fences, a technique revealed to me on a 1979 visit to China. The straw is poked into the sand in three-foot squares, leaving part of the straw sticking up above the sand. The resulting latticework breaks the force of the wind at ground level, stopping dune movement by confining the sand within the squares of the grid. The method has been used to tame a 24-mile corridor of shifting dunes along a railroad that links northwestern China with the eastern provinces. According to desert-research scientists at Lanzhou, the technique has served them well since 1958.

Later during that visit to China, I journeyed to the Turpan Oasis in Xinjiang Province, where I learned about another ingenious solution to a local problem. The oasis lies between the snowcapped Tian Shan mountains and the Turpan Depression, at 505 feet below sea level the lowest point in China. At the foot of the mountains, meltwater fans out onto talus slopes and disappears into them.

Uygur villagers living here long ago discovered they could dig down to the subterranean water and, by tunneling beneath the ground, could make use of gravity to bring water from the foothills into their fields to grow bountiful crops of melons, grapes, and vegetables. The Uygur call these under-

The glow of desert hospitality warms a Bedouin encampment in Saudi Arabia. Here a member of the Al Amrah clan prepares freshly roasted coffee after an evening meal of rice and lamb. In an environment where oases are widely scattered and summer temperatures climb to 120°F, hospitality may mean the difference between life and death. Bedouin custom decrees that even a sworn enemy may remain in camp for three days; to allow less would dishonor the family name. The harshness of desert life fostered strong kinship ties and tribal loyalty. Survival depended on it. Disloyalty could bring banishment— a punishment tantamount to a sentence of death.

38

Zebu bullocks share a ruminative moment at a fair in Pushkar, India. Every year tens of thousands of pilgrims and traders attend the week-long event in central Rajasthan, bathing in the holy waters of Pushkar Lake, haggling over livestock, and enjoying contests of strength and skill.

In Somalia a young nomad cradles a kid (above). Throughout the arid world, livestock forms the core of local economies, providing their owners with milk, meat, muscle power —and a source of pride.

40

Rewinding his 42-foot-long turban—called a pagri—*after dipping it in a nearby well, a herdsman in the Great Indian Desert protects his head from a blazing noonday sun.*

An African Wodaabe tribesman's turban (above) loops to protect nose and mouth from windblown sand.

NEXT PAGE: *Marching relentlessly from the Sahara, a wave of sand threatens to engulf a pasture in Niger's Sahel region. Some wind-driven dunes can travel up to a foot a day.*

ground irrigation channels *karez.* Nearly identical systems are called *qanats* in Iran and *aflaj* in Oman.

The desert regions we know today were not always harsh and inhospitable. Between 8000 and 3000 B.C., a much milder, moister climate prevailed in the Sahara. Rock paintings, graves, hand axes, and other archaeological evidence abound in the middle of a wasteland that today barely sustains snakes and lizards. The Sahara once bloomed with lime and olive trees, oaks and oleanders. Elephants, rhinos, gazelles, giraffes—and people—refreshed themselves in stream-fed pools and lakes. Similar lush conditions prevailed about 25,000, 60,000, and 200,000 years ago. Between moist periods came periods of dryness much like today's. These climatic fluctuations also appear to have occurred much earlier in Earth's history—perhaps as long as 720 million years ago, during the Precambrian. Most of today's deserts, however, are geologically young—about five million years old.

It is short-term climate swings that most affect human attempts to settle the arid lands, particularly along the semiarid fringes of the deserts where the environmental balance is fragile. Rainy years encourage people to settle; their herds quickly multiply—as do rodents, insects, and other pests. Then, when a succession of dry years returns, famine sets in, devastating plants, animals, and humans.

Such is the case now in the North African Sahel region, normally a semiarid seasonal grassland 200 to 700 miles wide that borders the southern edge of the Sahara. Throughout the Sahel rainfall is scanty and varies widely from season to season and place to place. Nomads long have pastured their herds on its sparse grasses, which seemed suitable for little else.

Before the 1940s, inhabitants of the Sahel freely roamed vast tracts of land in search of pastures. During dry spells they drifted southward to find greener grasses for their herds, knowing that the desert could move swiftly to reclaim more land for its dunes. The boundaries of the Sahara once extended nearly 200 miles farther south than they do today. Scientists have uncovered dunes

43

45

in Mali and Niger formed 20,000 years ago that are now stabilized by vegetation.

In the 1950s and '60s the movement of nomads gradually became curtailed as newly independent nations set up boundaries and began to restrict the free flow of goods along ancient trade routes and the seasonal movement of herds across national boundaries. Tuareg traders from Algeria, for example, no longer could pass freely into Niger. Local governments also began to settle nomads so they could be monitored and counted, and so schools, clinics, and aid from overseas could reach them.

The restriction of movement encouraged settlement. Farmers moved onto marginal lands; herders had their grazing domains strictly delineated. Irrigation projects, including deep borehole wells, made water available year-round—and encouraged herders to overgraze their ranges.

Then, beginning in the late 1960s, a series of droughts brought famine and illness to large parts of the Sahel. Destitute herders flocked to already overcrowded cities such as Nouakchott, Timbuktu, and Gao. Their children grew up in squalor and, like the children of Sheikh Al-Rashed, they never learned the ways of the desert.

The devastation made headlines around the world. With the headlines came the ungainly term "desertification." The term defines the impoverishment of arid and semiarid ecosystems by the actions of man. But the blame does not belong to herders alone. Indeed, these nomads may be responsible for whatever stability and sustainable productivity exists in their land.

Ecologists studying the Turkana people of Kenya have concluded that, given room to roam, these nomads and their cattle did not degrade the land. The same conclusion was reached by a Tufts University study of nomads in Niger. In short, restricting the movement of pastoralists may well be the major factor leading to land abuse.

Irrigation, of course, can make a world of difference in any desert. I was astounded the first time I set eyes on the Imperial Valley of southern California. Nearly half a million acres of fertile soil lay within walking distance of the Imperial Sand Dunes, one of the largest active dune fields in the United States. A 12-month growing season enables farmers to raise two crops a year, an agricultural feat made possible by tapping the waters of the Colorado River through the All-American *(Continued on page 52)*

Water's magic touch brings bounty to the wastelands as Israeli scientists, using ancient and modern irrigation techniques, coax crops from the Negev desert. Near the ruins of Avdat (opposite), researchers have rebuilt 2,500-year-old walls, dams, and conduits to collect runoff from seasonal rains and channel it to terraced grids. Today these plots yield abundant grapes, almonds, apricots, pistachios, barley, and wheat.

At an experimental farm near Beersheba, drip irrigation delivers water—a drop at a time—directly to a seedling, thus saving water that might be lost to evaporation.

47

A harmony of convergent hot-houses catches the rising sun on a cooperative farm near the Dead Sea in Israel. Plastic tunnels shelter salt-tolerant melons, tomatoes, and eggplants nurtured by brackish water. By slowing evaporation, the coverings help to curb salt buildup in the soil.

In Beersheba, agronomists acclimatize imported plants before testing them for hardiness in the Negev. A greenhouse worker (above) sprays tomatoes with fungicide, and edible cacti grow hydroponically.

49

In the thirsty southwestern United States, politicians and engineers tap rivers to quench demands for water. At Rancho Mirage (right), an oasis of wealth in the desert lands of southern California, a 242-mile aqueduct carries water from the Colorado River for irrigation—and for swimming pools and golf courses.

Near Sun City, Arizona, workers install concrete pipes (above) for a controversial project to tap the Colorado yet again with a 337-mile channel to Phoenix and Tucson. Its tunnels, canals, and giant pumps are built to siphon more than 3,000 cubic feet of water a second from a man-made reservoir called Lake Havasu.

Canal system. About 350,000 tons of lettuce comes from the Imperial Valley each year.

Desert agriculture is not always successful. It can damage the land permanently, particularly by excessive salinization. I have seen irrigated farmlands from Asia to America that were ruined by the use of brackish water without good drainage. Today, the development of proper drainage techniques and the search for salt-resistant crops provide hope for using such groundwater resources without ruining the land.

Pumping groundwater from aquifers also worries environmentalists. In Arizona and in Egypt's Western Desert, such water has accumulated over millennia and under wetter climates. Its continued use at present rates threatens depletion; rainfall cannot recharge the aquifers fast enough. Wells run dry and the land subsides.

But space-age technology may help solve this problem. Groundwater accounts for perhaps 95 percent of all the fresh, unfrozen water in the world—20 times more than in all the lakes, streams, and rivers. Much of this water lies in deep "fracture-zone" aquifers. Photographs taken from space reveal potential sources of water and modern drilling equipment can provide access to it. Not far from Tug Wajale in drought-plagued northwestern Somalia such methods have already yielded nearly two million gallons a day where none had been found before.

Water pumped in great quantities is crucial to the survival of the world's desert cities, whether Riyadh, Saudi Arabia, or Phoenix, Arizona, or the copper-rich mining towns of South America's Atacama Desert.

No matter how much we build and farm and mine and graze, we must remember to listen to the dry land, to touch it, to sense its changing moods. Our technological advances cannot totally replace our arid-land heritage. We must also learn to live in harmony with the desert, for the desert will be here long after we have wrung the last drop of oil from the sand.

A modern Saudi Arabian aphorism sums up the situation precisely: "My father rode a camel. I drive a car. My son will pilot a very expensive jet airplane. But my grandson, ah, my grandson, he will ride a camel."

52

FAROUK EL-BAZ

Off-highway vehicles scrawl environmental insults across the dunes of southern California's Sonoran Desert. Weekends bring as many as 40,000 visitors from nearby metropolises. Though a large part has been set aside to protect vulnerable plant and animal species, trail bikes and dune buggies range freely over more than 60 percent of the 304-square-mile area. Shifting sands periodically expose other evidence of man's presence: Live ammunition left from the days when U. S. Navy fliers practiced bombing runs on the dunes. Rainfall averages less than two inches a year here—not nearly enough to erase the indelible messages man too often inscribes in the fragile desert soil.

LIVING IN THE
ARCTIC

The great walrus bull slept soundly on a slab of ice, adrift in the dark, chill water. It did not hear the approaching hunters. Utuniarssuaq, a Polar Inuit from the Thule region of northwestern Greenland, guided our boat skillfully through the loose pack ice, keeping the outboard motor at its softest purr. His two partners from this northernmost community in the world stood in the bow, tense with excitement, rifles ready, a heavy, ivory-tipped walrus harpoon close at hand.

We were ten yards from the walrus when it awoke and reared up. The guns crashed; the great bull slumped and, with one final twist, slid off the ice. Kaigungnaaq thrust the harpoon into the animal just before it sank out of reach. We had the walrus now, but it seemed impossible for four men to haul the one-ton body back onto the ice, where we could cut it up into food for the men's families and sled dogs.

Utuniarssuaq made parallel cuts in the inch-thick skin on the walrus's neck. Then he chipped the ice into a line of pegs shaped like eyebolts, oiled a long sealskin thong with walrus blubber, and reeved it between the pegs and the skin flaps. While one man rocked the walrus to ease it over the edge of the floe, three of us hauled the walrus out of the water, our strength multiplied by this simple block and tackle.

Recently I lived with another group of Inuit (a name many of them prefer to Eskimo) more than 2,000 miles west of Thule: the beluga hunters of Kugmallit Bay at the edge of the Mackenzie River Delta in Canada. For ten months each year Alex Aviugana is a building contractor in the town of Inuvik, and his brother Rudolph runs an electrical contracting business. In summer they leave their comfortable homes in town and return "to the land," as people say in the north, to live in tents on the edge of shallow, turbid Kugmallit Bay, where Inuit have hunted white whales for hundreds, perhaps thousands, of years.

While distant icebreakers carried equipment to 200-million-dollar oil-drilling rigs in the Beaufort Sea, Alex returned from a hunt with the first whale of the season. Everyone in camp rushed to the beach to haul the whale ashore, an easy job as long as the whale was buoyed by water. But the moment the carcass struck gravel, it would not budge. Alex and Rudolph spiraled a strong Manila rope around the body and so, with a trick older than Archimedes, we rolled the whale close to the beach.

I have lived with Inuit, Aleuts, and Lapps for more than 30 years; their ingenuity never fails to amaze me. To survive in their northern realm, they have to be ingenious and hardy, adaptable and self reliant. Of all the regions inhabited by man, I consider the Arctic the harshest. One summer when I lived with Polar Inuit narwhal hunters at Inglefield Bay, the sea ice broke up on July 13—and on August 10 we had the first snowstorm of approaching autumn.

When you fly over the Arctic, you are overwhelmed by its vastness and the forbidding grandeur of its mountains and glaciers. And you think, surely no one can exist down there. Still, there is human life, tiny pockets of humanity scattered over the immensity of the north. Ellesmere Island, nearly the size of Great Britain, has a population of 114. The 72,000 people of Canada's Northwest and Yukon Territories could easily fit into a stadium, yet they inhabit a region larger than western Europe.

Hundreds of miles may separate ancient campsites, as with today's settlements and towns. But from eastern Greenland to the Bering Strait, a distance of 5,000 miles if you follow the coast that is home and highway to most arctic people, the Inuit are linked by a common language (with many regional dialects), a common heritage, and shared traditions and legends.

In Siorapaluk, Greenland, I watched an Inuit woman make cat's cradle figures with string. While her nimble fingers made one complex figure after another, her husband explained their meaning. One figure intrigued me. My host called it *kiligfagssuk*. "It means an animal. A very big animal. It existed a long time ago. Even the oldest people have never seen it."

I have watched Inuit in Canada's central Arctic make the identical figure. They call it *kilivaiciaq*. It represents the woolly mammoth. An echo from the dawn of man, the memory of this long-extinct arctic elephant

An Inuit hunter catches a meal of dovekies as millions of the chunky seabirds swirl above their nesting grounds on the Greenland coast. In a region too cold and rainless for farms or orchards, a diet of birds, mammals, and fish gives arctic dwellers the nutrients they need to survive. Today they live in two worlds but belong to neither—the traditional world of their forebears and the modern world of prefab houses, snowmobiles, politics, oil pipelines, and outsiders lured north by mineral riches and high wages.

PREVIOUS PAGE: Lantern glow gilds a Greenland Inuit and his igloo, a temporary hut built of snow blocks for a few nights' shelter on a trek.

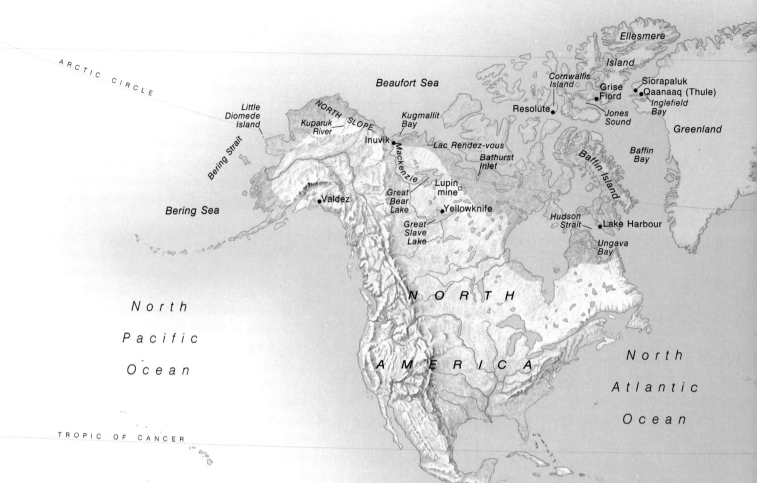

A r c t i c

Arctic

Ellesmere
Island

Cornwallis
Island
Grise
Fiord
Siorapaluk
Qaanaaq (Thule)
Inglefield
Bay

Resolute

Jones
Sound

Greenland

Beaufort Sea

Little
Diomede
Island

Kugmallit
Bay

NORTH SLOPE

Kuparuk
River

Inuvik

Mackenzie

— *Lac Rendez-vous*

Bathurst
Inlet

Baffin
Bay

Bering Strait

Baffin Island

Lupin
mine

Great
Bear
Lake

Yellowknife

Bering Sea

Valdez

Great
Slave
Lake

Hudson
Strait
Lake Harbour

Ungava
Bay

N o r t h

P a c i f i c

O c e a n

N O R T H

A M E R I C A

N o r t h

A t l a n t i c

O c e a n

ARCTIC CIRCLE

TROPIC OF CANCER

EQUATOR   0°

S O U T H

A M E R I C A

TROPIC OF CAPRICORN

S o u t h

P a c i f i c

O c e a n

Tierra
del Fuego

The Frozen Northlands

*Ice, snow, tundra, and rock
cover the lands rimming the
Arctic Ocean, where the tilt of
Earth's axis spins an intricate,
fragile web of existence. In
winter the sun disappears for
weeks or months, depending
on latitude. In summer even
the midnight sun—its rays at
an angle, never directly overhead—cannot thaw the permanently frozen ground. The
tundra's thin soil, underlain by
this permafrost, can support
only lichens and mosses, grasses and small plants, and a few
stunted trees. Precipitation*

*averages just ten inches a year,
making the Arctic a frigid desert. Temperatures often fall to
−40°F in winter, when winds
blast unhindered across the ice-
bound seas and treeless land.*

*Clearly this region would
seem unfit for human habita-
tion. And yet, people have lived
here thousands of years, people
who adapted to the Arctic's
rigors and learned to use its
bountiful wildlife, people who
call this majestic wilderness*
nunassiaq, *the beautiful land.*

Northern Tundra and Ice

58

Ocean

Iceland

Ocean

Chukchi
Peninsula

Bering Strait

Big
Diomede
Island

Bering Sea

SAAMILAND
(LAPLAND)

SCANDINAVIA

S   I   B   E   R   I   A

• Novgorod

Lake
Baykal

North

EUROPE

Pacific

Chernobyl •

A   S   I   A

Ocean

AFRICA

Indian Ocean

AUSTRALIA

South

Atlantic

Ocean

survives in a single string figure of Inuit storytellers half a continent apart.

To survive in the Arctic, the Inuit and other northern peoples have evolved over thousands of years a life-style almost perfectly adapted to cold. Our furless skin tells us that we humans were originally designed for a warm climate. We certainly are a cold-sensitive species, biologically ill suited for life in the Arctic. A naked human, exposed to −40°F temperature and 40-mile-an-hour wind, conditions not unusual in the north, will freeze to death in minutes.

Despite this handicap, the Neandertals spread northward through Europe about 125,000 years ago. Their Cro-Magnon successors, who lived from 35,000 until 10,000 years ago during Europe's last major ice age, perfected many Neandertal tools and weapons and developed an arsenal of new ones that made them the master hunters of their icy age: the spear-thrower, still used by the Polar Inuit to increase the distance a harpoon can be hurled; the harpoon, still an essential tool of arctic sea mammal hunters; iron pyrite stones, used with flint to produce sparks and fire; and perhaps the fish weir and the bow and arrow.

Equally important was the invention of the needle, which helped the Cro-Magnons make finely tailored clothes. This protective shell insulated them from the lethal cold.

An experienced Inuit seamstress can take the measure of her man at a glance and produce clothing that will make him nearly impervious to winter weather: inner and outer parka and pants of caribou fur; sealskin or caribou boots; disposable insoles of dried grass; down-soft socks of arctic hare skin; and caribou fur mittens with sealskin palms for extra strength. The entire suit is airy and light—about ten pounds—and so warm that a hunter can walk comfortably all day in a breeze at −40°F.

Proof of this came to me on a seal hunt near Thule. My Inuit companion and I traveled all day by dog team to the limit of land-fast ice and waited in vain all night for seals. I was cold and hungry, but he had brought no food; that would have reflected badly on

Awaiting the carving knife, walrus carcasses proclaim a successful hunt in the Thule region of northwestern Greenland. The massive beasts— weighing as much as 1.5 tons each—will provide meat and blubber for the Inuit and their dogs, as well as teeth and tusks for tools and ornamental carvings. Little is wasted.

Protected by law, walrus may be hunted only by Inuit and Aleuts, and only for their own use.

his ability as a hunter. (He shot a seal the next night—our first meal in 36 hours.) I was all for setting up tent and sleeping. "No tent," he said. It was April and –20°F—really quite warm, he explained. With that he curled up on the sled and, dressed in traditional fur clothing, slept soundly and warmly while I, in my expensive "arctic" sleeping bag, shivered for a long, long time.

Warmly dressed prehistoric people began to migrate from Siberia 25,000 or 30,000 years ago, crossing the land bridge that linked Asia and America during much of the Pleistocene. Over millennia these ancestors of today's Indians fanned out across North America and down into South America, all the way to Tierra del Fuego.

The Inuit forebears, coming across about 6,000 years ago, spread slowly eastward, 5,000 miles across the harsh tundra at the top of the North American Continent to Greenland. Some settled as far north as northern Ellesmere Island, less than 600 miles from the North Pole.

Theirs was a demanding realm. Winters were long, dark, and cold; summers short, cool, and often mosquito plagued. They lacked the raw materials that other societies considered essential. Wood was rare in much of the Arctic, so rare that in a few areas Inuit sometimes made sleds out of long strips of frozen meat lashed together with thong. Such sleds were serviceable and, in emergencies, could be eaten. Metal—native copper and meteoric iron—was found only in a few isolated localities.

That left most Inuit with snow, ice, stone, and sod. Vitally important, then, were materials from animals: skins for clothing and bedding, sinew for thread, intestines for waterproof clothing and sails, seal leather for boot soles and thimbles, musk-ox horn for blubber pounders and spoons.

Despite the odds—a deadly climate, few raw materials, little contact with other societies—the Inuit developed one of the most complex technologies of any preindustrial people. Today they adapt modern gadgets and conveniences to their age-old ways.

Once, while camped at the edge of a floe with a Polar Inuit and his wife, waiting for seal and hoping for narwhal or beluga, I inventoried some of the things on their dogsled: a canvas tent; caribou sleeping skins, mattresses, and a large sealskin to spread beneath them for insulation; three rifles and ammunition; an ivory-tipped seal harpoon and much *(Continued on page 71)*

In the blustery cold of northwestern Greenland, Inuit hunters haul a harpooned seal onto the ice. Elsewhere in the Arctic, rifles have largely replaced harpoons, but Inuit women still use the traditional ulu—*woman's knife—to clean sealskin. The women stretch the hides to dry in the sun, then make them into boot soles, pants and parkas, thongs, and dog harnesses.*

NEXT PAGE: *Colorful costume proclaims the regional homeland of a Saami reindeer herder. Called Lapps by outsiders, the 40,000 Saami of the Scandinavian Arctic struggle to maintain their identity in a world where alcohol, assimilation, and government policies threaten traditional ways.*

A moving fence of burlap and wire mesh drives reindeer into corrals during spring roundup in Norway. In a three-day task that is also a major social event, Saami herders bring the animals from tundra wintering grounds to be sorted, counted, and then escorted to coastal or highland summer pastures. Vaccination (left), expensive but compulsory in Finland, helps protect the deer from fly larvae, which can lodge in their throats and cause suffocation.

Although more and more Saami are taking salaried jobs, the number of deer is increasing. Overcrowding strains their food resources—and perhaps their psyches: Reindeer are now found to have stomach ulcers.

67

Freeze-dried by Finland's cold winter, reindeer jerky serves as trail food for the Saami. The herder at right skins the carcasses of newly slaughtered animals. Like the walrus and seals vital to the Inuit, reindeer provide the Saami with pelts for clothing and tents, and meat for a high-energy diet rich in fat and protein. But in parts of northern Scandinavia, fallout from the Chernobyl nuclear plant contaminated the lichen on which reindeer feed, making their meat and milk unsafe for humans.

heavier whale and walrus harpoons; coils of nylon rope and bearded-seal thong as spare harpoon lines and as cords to lash the load onto the sled; large hooks and a gaff to catch Greenland halibut; a long-handled scoop net to capture the chubby, starling-size dovekies; a fully equipped, sealskin-covered kayak; a steel-tipped ice chisel; two Primus stoves; a jerrycan of kerosene; matches; pliers; screwdrivers; binoculars; a sewing kit with narwhal sinew as thread; a patch kit of assorted fur pieces and leather; spare sealskin boots; rubber boots; four cooking pots and an enameled chamber pot; a cordless shaver . . . even Donald Duck comic books in Danish. Thus equipped, we could have traveled and lived off land and sea for weeks or even months.

The people know every detail of their land and navigate across it with uncanny accuracy. An Inuit friend and I once traveled by dog team in a snowstorm across Jones Sound in Canada's high Arctic. We did not have a compass. In a world all white, we kept a course due south by crossing the *sastrugi*—snow ripples laid down by the prevailing east-west winds—at right angles. During a brief lull in the storm, we saw the

Using sinew for thread, a Canadian Inuit creates a traditional caribou-skin parka. Such ancient crafts help support modern Inuit. Carving, once limited to weapons, tools, and a few toys, has become a major source of income. Fine pieces, like this soapstone hunter brandishing an ivory harpoon, command high prices.

vague outline of a cliff in the distance. My friend recognized it instantly, although it was years since he had seen it.

The people of the north are guided by millennia of passed-on experience and wisdom. They can recognize where strong currents have weakened the ice; they watch the raven's flight, for it may lead them to polar bears or caribou herds; they know the signs that presage storms.

Once, in the Bering Strait between Alaska and Siberia, I took part in a walrus hunt with a group of villagers from Little Diomede Island. We set out in perfect weather in a skin boat called an umiak. Such days are rare in this region; fog and storms are far more normal. But on this day the sea was satin smooth as we weaved past wave-sculptured ice floes, white, turquoise, and emerald, mirrored in the dark water.

We had traveled for two hours when, without warning, someone shouted. Instantly our captain turned the umiak around and headed back for Little Diomede. "Why?" I asked. He pointed to a small lenticular cloud far to the west. "Big storm coming," he said. I couldn't believe it. The Little Diomeders are some of the most daring walrus hunters in Alaska and routinely set out in almost any weather.

But now we were racing home, blinded by hissing spindrift. We slipped behind Big Diomede Island on the Soviet side, then angled over to Little Diomede, where the men in the village helped us get the umiak ashore. Soaked by violent surf, shouting above the eldritch screeching of the wind, we had barely made it through the worst storm of the year.

In the past, furs were the greatest wealth of the Eurasian north. More than a thousand years ago, an Arab merchant-diplomat by the name of Ibn Fadhlan traveled, partly by dog team, to the famous fur fair at Novgorod in northern Russia to purchase the marvelous furs of Russia and Siberia: deep brown marten and mink, smoke gray vair and lustrous sable, and occasionally even a polar bear skin. Ibn Fadhlan was impressed by the men who brought furs from the far north: "As soon as the hunter buckles

71

boards eight or nine ells long to his feet, he conquers . . . greyhounds in running. . . ." The hunters had come on skis.

The most highly prized furs still come from the northern Soviet Union and from Canada. But in the Eurasian north, reindeer herding is infinitely more important. The Saami (or Lapps, as they have commonly been called) of Scandinavia and the Chukchi, Evenks, Yakuts, and other Siberian people are reindeer herders. Herding in some regions has become big business. Siberia has more than 2,000,000 reindeer; the Chukchi alone, in the Soviet Union's farthest east, herd about 700,000 animals. The meat and pelts are of enormous value, and antlers in velvet are sold throughout the

Orient as a valued aphrodisiac.

But herding never spread past the Bering Strait to any great extent. The Inuit were, and are, hunters.

Whether to hunter or herder, change has come rapidly in recent years. In the 1950s, when I began to live with the Inuit, most people were still on the land, hunting, fishing, and trapping at ancestral camps. (One site has been inhabited almost continuously for 4,000 years.) They lived in tents in summer; in winter, double-layered tents, snowhouses, or sod-and-stone huts. All the hunters had dog teams. Now most Inuit live in settlements and towns, in government-built houses of three or four bedrooms, or in apartment (Continued on page 79)

Dogs by the dozen pull a sledge and driver in Greenland; open terrain allows this fan formation. Once a mainstay of travel, dog teams have all but vanished in much of the north, replaced by the "gasoline dog" —the faster but costlier snowmobile. To buy one, a herder like the Norwegian Saami above must sell off reindeer.

NEXT PAGE: Founded as a weather station in 1947, the Canadian village of Resolute shelters 150 Inuit in buildings made of imported wood.

Age-old skill turns hard-packed snow into a snug winter shelter. After marking a circle in the snow, an Inuit uses a modern handsaw to cut wedge-shaped blocks, then stacks and trims these snow bricks into a compact, spiraling dome. One man can build a small igloo in about an hour.

The igloo's domed shape deflects icy winds; air pockets in the blocks of snow act as insulation to conserve heat. The body warmth of the occupants raises the temperature inside by about 40°. A low entrance tunnel slopes upward to keep the warmed air from escaping.

Though igloos were common only in the Canadian Arctic, they have become the universal symbol of the Inuit.

77

buildings. Only a few camps remain, yet, oddly, just when everyone predicted their demise, the number of camps is increasing. Social problems in the cities appall many Inuit; a few have moved permanently back to the land. Many spend at least the summer hunting and fishing, for, as one told me, "this is really our life."

Dog teams have nearly vanished. Snowmobiles, expensive but efficient, have taken their place, and today young Inuit dream of owning ever faster and bigger machines. Herders, too, use snowmobiles to stay with their animals during the extensive spring and fall migrations of the reindeer.

Despite machines and modernization, the elemental problems of the herder's life remain. Two brothers from Norwegian Saamiland (Lapland) took me along on the spring migration from the interior, where the reindeer had grazed in winter, to the coast, where their animals would spend summer on an island. We were on the bleak tundra plateau when a snowstorm began. The drifts rose and the 1,700 reindeer, the brothers' entire wealth, seemed to vanish into a white void. It was the nightmare of the Saami, to have his herd scattered in a blizzard. While I waited in the *kåta,* a conical tent, the men were out in the storm, trying to contain the herd. Occasionally one of the brothers returned, coated in snow and rime, haggard with fatigue. He would cut off chunks of dried reindeer meat with his *buiko,* the curved Saami dagger, and gulp them down in a hurry, drink strong coffee from an age-blackened wooden cup, and head out into the storm again. At times the men did not sleep for 50 hours, and 30 of their animals (they seemed to know all 1,700) were never seen again.

To the old problems of snow, storms, and scattering herds, problems peculiar to our age have been added. *Cladonia* lichens, the reindeer's main food, usually called reindeer moss or caribou moss, absorb radioactive particles from the air, including fallout from atomic testing. These cancer-causing particles accumulate in the reindeer's tissues. After the nuclear disaster

at Chernobyl in 1986, cesium levels in Swedish reindeer meat soared to 77 times the safe levels established by Swedish health authorities. The Saami, who normally eat eight to ten reindeer a year, can now neither eat the meat nor sell it. (The Swedish government has bought the contaminated meat and gives it to mink and fox farms.) "We have been reindeer herders for 2,000 years," said one herder. "If we have to give it up now, the [Saami] culture will die."

Buffeted by the winds of change, the Saami and other natives of the north have shown amazing resilience and ingenuity. In the 1950s and '60s, as more and more villages and towns were built in the north by the Canadian government, Inuit left the land and settled in these new centers. But the area around settlements was soon hunted out, and there was little employment. As a result, many Inuit became artists, and their art became world famous.

Inuit lithographs, drawings, paintings, silk-screen prints and, above all, soapstone carvings range from simple craftsmanship to inspired artistry, the inspiration derived from the legends and lore of a hunting past. The best pieces are in great museums and private collections all over the world.

Bundled in a snowsuit of reindeer fur, a Siberian child toddles off from her home—a tent made of reindeer skins stretched over wood poles. More skins carpet the twigs, bark, and grasses that insulate the tent floor. Woolen blankets cover the birch framework of the Norwegian Saami herder's tent at left. Such portable homes, quickly erected and dismantled, enable herders to follow the seasonal wanderings of the reindeer. Few herders now use tents year-round, living instead in government-built houses in permanent settlements that spring up as nations develop the Arctic's coal, oil, and natural gas. Reindeer herding in Soviet Siberia is now collectivized on state farms.

Ekalun of the Umingmakturmiut, whose tent I shared for the six and a half months I lived with these musk-ox people of Canada's Bathurst Inlet, still remembered the day he had been "discovered" by white explorers on a 1913-18 expedition. Their sleds were laden with treasures such as steel knives and needles, precious to a people who made knives of cold-hammered native copper and needles of the wing bones of gulls and geese. Until then Ekalun had hunted caribou with a bow of carved and pegged-together pieces of driftwood, backed with plaited sinew for strength, the whole tightly wrapped with sealskin. Such a bow was a marvel of ingenuity but a poor weapon. For a sure shot Ekalun had to crawl within about 20 paces of a caribou.

By the time we met, he owned guns, a 22-foot canoe, an outboard motor, a radio that brought to our remote camp the news of the world, and a Swiss watch. Much of this he had paid for by selling carvings. His specialty was chess sets, the board inlaid and bordered with polished stones of many colors. The rooks were igloos, the knights polar bears, the bishops dogs, the pawns a little army of obese arctic owls. King and queen were Inuit in full fur regalia.

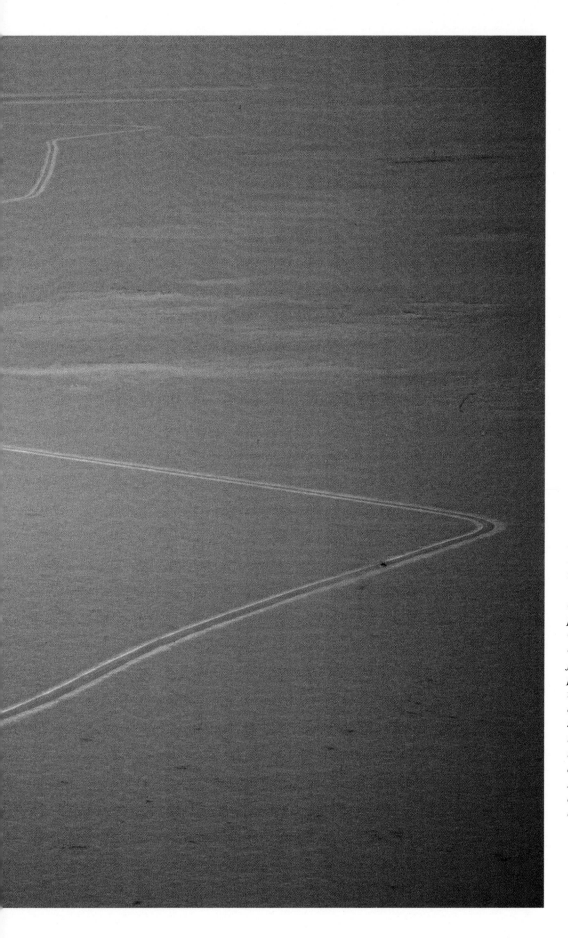

Trucks skid in a behemoth ballet on the icy road between Yellowknife and the Lupin gold mine in Canada's Northwest Territories. Remade each year by specially equipped snowplows, the 370-mile, winter-only road zigzags mainly across the six-foot-thick ice of frozen lakes. Airplanes transport people and supplies year-round, but the winter road allows cheaper delivery of fuel, supplies, and equipment. The trucks, weighing as much as 50 tons when fully loaded, travel at 20 miles an hour or less. During the two-day journey, drivers can sleep, eat, and shower at rest stops along the way.

Eighty feet down, hoarfrost decorates an unused passageway in the Lupin gold mine (opposite). Miners drilled and blasted 1,770 feet to the bottom of permafrost, then continued another 760 feet to the mine shaft's present depth. In a world far different from the cold and empty land above, a worker at 800 feet (right, upper) drills holes in preparation for blasting. In a refinery at the surface, another worker tends the smelting furnace as molten doré bullion, a gold-and-silver alloy, pours into a slag pot. About 450 people work here, most in twelve-hour shifts of two weeks on, two weeks off. In 1986 the Lupin mine produced 193,200 ounces of gold—then worth almost $71,000,000.

83

One day Ekalun's watch stopped. He handed it to me. "You fix it," he said. I recoiled. That was a job for a watch repairman. Ekalun laughed and began to take the watch apart. The tools he lacked, he made: tiny screwdrivers patiently filed from darning needles. Before evening he had assembled the watch again—and it worked.

Many Inuit oscillate between disparate worlds. They work for weeks or months at one of the new mines in the north, then leave to hunt or work as artists for several weeks. Traditional food sources are skillfully exploited. In April and May the people of Ungava Bay—which has one of the highest tides in the world—wait until the tide falls away from the ice near shore, then crawl beneath the ceiling of ice to collect mussels by the pailful. On Little Diomede Island in spring the people use small bone mattocks to dig up the corms of the spring beauty flower. They look like tiny potatoes and are eaten with seal oil.

In June people from Lake Harbour on Baffin Island travel to the remote Savage Islands in Hudson Strait to collect eider eggs—a custom now forbidden by Canadian authorities. The two families with whom I went practiced an ancient Inuit form of conservation by visiting only a few of the breeding islands, while on the other islands the eiders incubated their eggs in peace. We came home after a week with 3,000 eggs. The Inuit ate the cracked eggs at once and stored the rest in shady rock niches.

P ast and future strangely intermingle in the Arctic. Recently I met a young Inuit in western Canada. In summer he worked for an oil company on one of those futuristic exploration rigs in the Beaufort Sea. The rig's great room, full of computer banks, looked like the command post of a space vehicle. In autumn the young man left his well-paid job, chartered a plane, and flew with his family to Lac Rendez-vous, more than a hundred miles from the nearest settlement. There they lived all winter and spring in a log cabin, hunting, trapping, and fishing, combining in their existence the Arctic of the past with the Arctic of the future.

FRED BRUEMMER

Steel beams lift the trans-Alaska pipeline above the tundra on a zigzag route that minimizes earthquake damage. Completed in 1977, the 800-mile pipeline brings two million barrels of North Slope oil daily to the terminal at Valdez (right). Facing bitter opposition from environmentalists, the pipeline's builders met the challenge of safely conveying the heated oil. Almost half the line is buried— and cooled with refrigerants to keep it from thawing the permafrost. More pipelines may soon tap the Arctic's mineral wealth.

LIVING ON
ISLANDS

You can already tell a lot about the islanders up ahead, just by approaching their land as any voyager did until this century—by sea. From your rolling deck, even before their home rises on the horizon, clues tell you that these particular islanders probably live on a lush, well-watered isle of limited size. They are most likely descended from a great seafaring race. For much of their history they were little touched by foreign contact. Now, though, they are especially vulnerable to it.

As the island itself pokes above the horizon, you can see it should produce enough food for all, year-round, provided the islanders have dealt with the danger of overcrowding. You also suspect that a lot of their foreign contact is with tourists.

Much of this is easy to guess. Just by the several weeks it took to sail here, you could tell that only experienced seafarers would have reached this place. Having settled it, they would remain isolated from any but equally good seafarers, at least until air travel changed island life forever. But you might need an experienced eye to recognize the first sign of the island itself: not land, but cumulus clouds above it. "Clouds getting caught on the mountaintop," as these islanders would say—a sign of rain-soaked slopes beneath. The clouds do not spread very far, so neither does the island.

When the mountains themselves appear, their steep, eroded volcanic slopes promise rich soil below. And when you see waves breaking on the island's surrounding coral reef, you know this is a climate that invites year-round agriculture—and visitors. The lovely scenery must attract tourists, who seek the escape of remoteness but who arrive in the jetliners that conquer it.

A gap in the reef lets you pass into the still lagoon, and a wall of greenery flecked by many white balconies confronts you. No building in this port city exceeds the height of the the coconut palms. In fact, local policy keeps it that way, for you have made landfall on an island where beauty itself is an economic resource: Tahiti.

I have visited many such islands in my voyaging career and have seen how critical a resource can be, particularly in remote locations. For on any island, the barrier of the surrounding sea imposes limits that define the nature of island life. How easy, how hard, is that barrier to cross? How easy *should* it be?

This absolute watery frontier, historian Jacquetta Hawkes has written, "gives island people a sharp awareness of their identity and of their difference from everyone else. Even today in the Isle of Wight, a modest patch of land fitting close to the English shore, people from the mainland are called 'overners' and are regarded as inferior aliens." The mainland English for their part envisioned, as mainlanders will, island-as-paradise. Their 17th-century proverb portrayed a land with no predators: "The Isle of Wight hath no Monks, Lawyers, or Foxes."

The islander sense of identity once greeted me at both ends of an Atlantic crossing. Preparing to sail from Newfoundland, an island that did not join Canada until 1949, I almost got punched in St. John's, the capital. I had called some men on a ship at the wharf "you Canadians." "We're not Canadians; we're Newfies!" came the outraged reply.

I set sail, face still intact. When the clouds lifted at the end of my voyage, I saw the dark outline of the Shetlands rimming the horizon. In the Middle Ages these Scottish islands remained under Norse control for centuries longer than the Scottish mainland did. The effects have lingered. Shetlanders like to make the claim—almost true—that the nearest railway station lies not south in Scotland, but to the east in Bergen, Norway. Sounding a now familiar refrain, they told me, "We're na Scots; we're Norse!"—in a fine Scottish accent.

Coming from islands that are neither separate countries nor unusually remote, such attitudes underscore the oft-made observation that an island is "a world apart."

How far apart? How rich or poor a world? The answers set the two basic limits of island life: accessibility and resources. How to deal with them is up to the islanders.

They often deal in surprising ways. People on overcrowded islands, or with few resources, may be among the richest islanders, and those on a seeming paradise among the poorest. People of remote

A crowded islet in the southern Philippines takes typical island problems—limited space and resources—to the extreme. Dependent solely on fishing, villagers must go farther to sea as commercial and local over-fishing depletes stocks. Small islands are particularly vulnerable to such economic disruption; few resources leave fewer ways to respond to change.

PREVIOUS PAGE: *Fishermen off southwestern Madagascar speed along in technology tested by thousands of miles—and years. Seafarers in outrigger sailing canoes—large versions of these coastal pirogues—settled remote islands across much of the world centuries before European explorers set forth.*

Island Worlds

Countless islands stipple Earth's seas with variety: from isolated chunks of continent like Ireland and Greenland to Micronesia's sprinkle of tiny atolls. The volcanic, hilly Azores rise from roots deep in the ocean; the flat Bahamas from a barely submerged plateau. Big islands such as Java, Honshu, or Great Britain support tens of millions of people, while in the South Atlantic, windswept Bouvet— the most isolated bit of land on Earth—harbors only seals and seabirds. All these islands share just one thing: the protecting, confining, encircling water.

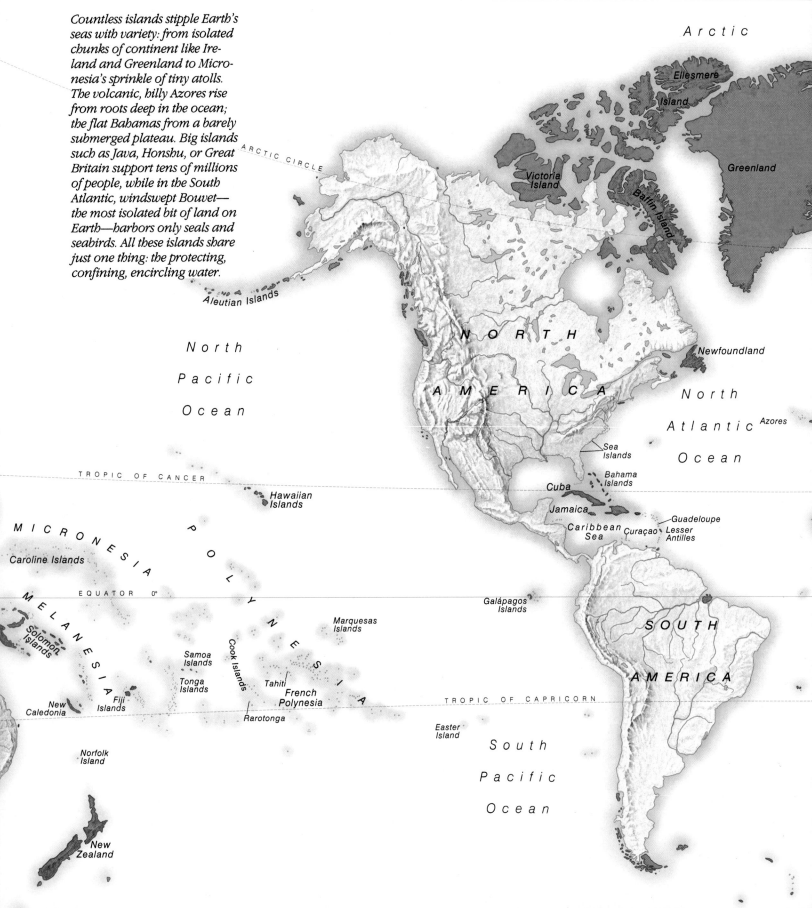

Arctic

Ellesmere Island

Greenland

Victoria Island

Baffin Island

ARCTIC CIRCLE

Aleutian Islands

NORTH AMERICA

Newfoundland

North Pacific Ocean

North Atlantic Ocean

Azores

Sea Islands

TROPIC OF CANCER

Hawaiian Islands

Bahama Islands

Cuba

Jamaica

Guadeloupe

MICRONESIA

Caribbean Sea

Curaçao

Lesser Antilles

Caroline Islands

POLYNESIA

MELANESIA

EQUATOR 0°

Galápagos Islands

SOUTH AMERICA

Solomon Islands

Marquesas Islands

Samoa Islands

Cook Islands

Tonga Islands

Tahiti

French Polynesia

New Caledonia

Fiji Islands

TROPIC OF CAPRICORN

Rarotonga

Easter Island

South Pacific Ocean

Norfolk Island

New Zealand

O c e a n

Svalbard

Iceland

Shetland
Islands

Heimaey

Hebrides

Great
Britain

Isle of
Wight

E U R O P E

A S I A

North

Pacific

Ocean

Honshu

Japan

Adriatic
Sea

Mediterranean Sea

Bahrain

Taiwan

Hong
Kong
Macau

A F R I C A

Andaman
Islands

M I C R O N E S I A

Caroline Islands

Sri
Lanka

Philippines

Singapore

M E L A N E S I A

Sumatra

Borneo

Celebes

Moluccas

New
Guinea

I N D O N E S I A

Solomon
Islands

Java

Madura

Madagascar

Indian Ocean

Fiji
Islands

New
Caledonia

Tristan da
Cunha Group

S o u t h

A U S T R A L I A

Norfolk
Island

A t l a n t i c

O c e a n

Bouvet
Island

Tasmania

New
Zealand

islands surmount isolation, while those living just offshore may thrive on it.

Much of what islanders do depends on just what type of island they live on.

Some islands are huge—sea-girded slabs of continental crust, such as Greenland, the world's biggest island. New Guinea holds second place. Flat maps of the world usually distort their size, enlarging Greenland and shrinking New Guinea. A globe shows both islands are about 1,500 miles long, the distance from California to the Mississippi.

Some other large islands are part continental, part volcanic, such as New Zealand or Japan. Mid-ocean seafloor volcanoes create many smaller islands: Hawaii, the Lesser Antilles, or Tristan da Cunha.

Some of these volcanic islands can grow with sudden speed, as I saw in the Azores. Eruptions just off the island of Faial in 1957 had added so much new land that Capelinhos Lighthouse, set on what was once a seaside cliff, now stood hidden from the sea in a valley behind ridges of basalt.

Different forces have raised a few islands in the Pacific, where centuries of seafaring have conditioned some islanders to think that islands themselves float. A Micronesian navigator, Hipour, told me about the island of Fais and the Pacific demigod Maui: "I have seen seashells embedded in the soil of the highest hill. How else could they have got there if Maui had not fished up Fais from under the sea?" The legend is not far from truth. A slow collision between crustal plates had forced Fais upward—a typical "raised reef" island.

"Moreover," Hipour continued, "the people of Yap have Maui's fishhook and have long threatened to sink the island again if we do not do their bidding." The Yapese, who held sway over much of Micronesia for centuries, did nothing to discourage the belief that if an island could float it could also sink, Yap willing.

In fact, many islands do slowly sink, Yap willing or not. Older ocean floor tends to subside as it creeps away from mid-ocean ridges, so any islands it bears sink with it.

Thus volcanism and seafloor subsidence account for many of the two kinds of islands known, in the Pacific especially, as "high" and "low." High islands—volcanic, fertile,

A deluge of lava and ash enlarges the island of Heimaey, off Iceland's southern coast, in 1973. The five-month eruption buried part of Vestmannaeyjar, Iceland's most important fishing port. A semimolten lava flow started to close the harbor. Islanders pumped hundreds of tons of water onto the creeping mass, helping to cool and divert it. With typical islander resourcefulness, they later ran water pipes through the hot, now hardened rock, to heat the town for decades to come. This eruption—like those that formed Iceland itself—originated within the globe-girdling Mid-Ocean Ridge. Earth's crustal plates separate along the ridge, creating new seafloor —and the occasional island.

mountainous, well watered—allow varied agriculture. Tahiti is one. With age, the island erodes. If it's on a subsiding seafloor, it sinks until little is left but the ever growing reef: a low island. Midway is one. Subject to drought and hurricane flooding, these infertile coral atolls are hard to farm. Low islanders depend heavily on fishing or outside aid. Much of Micronesia is low island.

Most fleeting of all are islands made of sediment. Sitting atop the continental shelf,

sandy barrier islands like those of North Carolina's Outer Banks move and reform with ocean currents and storms—as many a beach-cottage owner has painfully learned.

What do all the greatly varying kinds of islands have in common? Nothing—except for the barrier of water that makes an island an island. Like any wall, that barrier is two sided. It helps keep the world out; it helps keep the islanders in. It offers protection; it limits opportunity.

And like any wall, it can be crossed, given the right tools. Until this century, the tools were seagoing vessels. Since the coming of radio, airplane, and satellite TV dish, the islander's wall is lower than it used to be.

In places, the *(Continued on page 101)*

Fishermen of Madagascar's Vezo clan study the sea as sunrise gilds their waiting pirogues. The fleet enables them to make a living with net and spear along the island's inhospitably dry southwestern coast. Fitted with sails and oars, pirogues can navigate open water and coral reefs alike. On long trips, dismantled sails and rigging double as tents. A Vezo boy's first boat takes shape (above) under his father's experienced hands. Vezo craftsmen carve each pirogue from a single tree trunk.

Scaled, gutted, and impaled, the day's catch cooks around a Vezo bonfire. When golden brown and dried, the fish can be traded inland for manioc, corn, and sorghum.

On smaller islands, fishing may be vital—a prehistoric petroglyph of a willing catch (opposite, upper) bespeaks its importance to Easter Islanders, whose sheer cliffs and rough seas made fishing risky. For many islands, coral reefs offer a living larder, as a Vezo harpooner (lower) demonstrates.

NEXT PAGE: Following tradition, women and children of Sat-awal, Micronesia, collect sea urchins on the reef at low tide. Among coral islanders, men usually fish, women gather.

100

sea barrier is no more than a narrow strait or passage. Possibly its most humble use is by crofters of the Hebrides—as a sheep fence. These farmers move their sheep to nonarable islands for the summer, so the animals will have fresh pastures and won't get into the vegetable gardens back home.

More often a strait serves as a moat. Great Britain—an island so big it is "mainland" to the Isle of Wight—is only a long swim from Europe, but the English Channel has given the British both a measure of protection and an unarguable sense of identity.

Combine the moat with an excellent harbor located on a trade route, and you have a special class of islands. These are the urban marketplace isles—Singapore, Venice, Hong Kong and Macau, Bahrain, Manhattan, Montreal, and others. Often they grow fabulously wealthy with no resources other than their geography. Many, like Manhattan and Hong Kong, have now bridged their moats or tunneled under them, and overflowed so onto nearby lands that they are no longer really islands.

Siting a city on an island is an ancient impulse. The pre-Roman Phoenicians, great traders, built Tyre on one, which Alexander the Great later tied to the mainland with a causeway. The Venetians, also great traders, also liked islands. They built cities and forts on isles down the coast of the Adriatic and into the Aegean.

Without a harbor and a strategic location, offshore islands are unlikely to sprout great cities. They may, however, provide protected ground where distinctive societies and customs can prosper apart from the main. In the Sea Islands of Georgia and South Carolina, for example, emancipated slaves retained a way of life rich in song and folklore—the Gullah culture. Afro-American traditions that disappeared from the mainland survived here. Extended families still lived in houses around a common yard, and storytellers still spoke of Brer Rabbit and Brer Gator. In the Gullah dialect, a kind of creole with hundreds of colorful terms, the phrase you would use for "this island" perfectly evokes any islander's point of view: *this side.*

Gullah ways have begun to vanish under an onslaught of mass media, resort development, and disdain by young islanders. It is a common pattern: Impressed with the sophistication of newly accessible mainland society, island youths come to scorn their own more restricted backgrounds.

Even so, small islands may nurture and protect ways of life unknown on the mainland, taking on a cultural importance far greater than their size. The phenomenon can occur on large islands, too. Few Western nations, for instance, seem more distinctively a world apart than Iceland.

Part of it is physical. Approaching Iceland by sea, you might find clouds hanging low. From over choppy waves a chill wind blows mist in your face. Dark slopes of volcanic basalt bulk on the horizon under the gray ceiling. A fuzz of green fades partway up the low, flat-topped mountains, tapering off where the cold of altitude keeps grass from growing. This is summer—too chilly and short for raising many crops. Winters are long and dark, but relatively mild.

Such conditions forge interesting people. Icelanders would tell me what a calm, phlegmatic race they were, even as their eyes sparkled with excitement. They are not generally as tall or blond as their Scandinavian brethren on the mainland. When the Norse settled Iceland, around A.D. 900, they brought dark-haired Celtic slaves and Celtic wives with them—not to mention finding some Irish settlers already here.

The blood may be part Celtic, but Icelanders have retained a culture more Norse than that in the mainland Viking homelands of Norway, Sweden, or Denmark. One Icelander called his country "a sort of national park of Nordic culture."

The Althing, the parliament Iceland established in A.D. 930, survives today. Modeled on Norse local assemblies, it is the world's oldest national legislature. And only Iceland retains the Norse patronymic naming system. Anna Pétursdottir (daughter of Pétur), who does not change her name when she marries Magnus Jónsson (son of Jón), bears a son whom they might name Einar Magnússon.

No wonder that Icelandic telephone books list people by first name, not last.

The language itself has changed only a little from the time of settlement. Foreign

terms are discouraged in favor of Icelandic neologisms. In Swedish, microscope is *mikroskop;* in Icelandic *smásjá*—small-see. Modern Icelanders can still read Viking sagas in the original Old Norse.

And they do. Here the sagas live. I have heard staid Icelandic farmer-fishermen arguing whether Bjarni Herjólfsson was timid or sensibly prudent in A.D. 998 when, having lost his way on a late-season voyage to Greenland, he sighted North America— and turned away to head for the Greenland settlements, leaving it to his cousin Leifur Eiríksson to land in the New World. As a child in the South Pacific I had listened to stories of how the Maoris discovered New Zealand. Now I was hearing similar island-

Only a few feet away from the briny Pacific, Western Samoans enjoy a freshwater oasis (left). Fed by natural springs, the pool acts as a gathering place where villagers dip their jugs and entire families come to bathe. A dike of volcanic rocks prevents salt water from mixing with fresh. Less fortunate, a Vezo woman of south-western Madagascar (above) makes do at a brackish seaside well. Water scarcity in her dry region parallels that of small, porous coralline islands, which may have no sweet water at all.

er tales on this chill, far side of the globe.

Unlike the Maoris, though, Icelanders wrote their sagas down, mostly in the 12th and 13th centuries. Today this highly educated population continues to consume books like few others. One representative survey found that the average home has over 300 books in it, and that 27 percent of adults have published something. The long winters invite reading, and the Icelanders I met discussed literature in such depth as to make me feel a cultural ignoramus.

If the Sea Islands, just offshore, and Iceland, only a few hundred miles from Europe, have nurtured such unusual societies, it is easy to suppose that people on remote Pacific islands would differ even more from

one another. But that is not necessarily so.

Certainly there are variations. Cultural geographers divide the Pacific islands into three main regions, according to language groups, social customs, and racial characteristics: Polynesia, Micronesia, and Melanesia, which mean respectively "many islands," "small islands," and "islands of the blacks"—accurate descriptions. Melanesia, including New Guinea, has by far the most land area, comprising large islands at moderate distances from each other. Micronesia's small islets and atolls lie scattered across 4,000 miles of open ocean and add up to a land area no bigger than the state of Rhode Island. Many Polynesian islands are somewhat larger, but lie scattered even

"Go up the mountain and work the plantation; in the evening, paddle the canoe out and fish." Thus does a Samoan now in his 40s describe his days as a youth. Life remains much the same for a young boy (far left) in independent and largely agricultural Western Samoa. "Plantations"—plots of any size—yield coconut, cacao, and taro, a starchy tuber and mainstay of many South Pacific diets. Youths still tend taro above Pago Pago harbor in American Samoa (left), a United States territory since 1900. But plentiful American dollars make it easier to buy imported food. Dollars have also brought industry: Two U. S.-built canneries ship out a third of all the tuna that Americans eat.

farther apart, over a vast triangle defined by Hawaii, New Zealand, and Easter Island.

And yet Polynesians on Tahiti may have more in common with their Maori brethren in New Zealand, 2,500 miles away, than one neolithic tribe in New Guinea's rugged interior has with the next. The reason is simple: Remote islands depend on voyaging. It is how they were settled, and how they maintain cultural contact and trade with the outside. The ocean which isolates them is also a bridge. This principle is even written into the Constitution of the Federated States of Micronesia: "The seas bring us together, they do not separate us."

To be sure, a seafaring legacy does not mitigate the day-to-day isolation imposed by great distance. I spent several childhood years on Rarotonga, a miniature Tahiti in the Cook Islands. It was always a special occasion for us when a big ship came in from afar. We would go to welcome it, to see who would get off and what would be unloaded.

Years later I was often on the other end of the welcome, as when our sailboat had anchored a mile off one of the Solomons. Inside the main cabin, I looked up to see that each porthole had a little boy's face in it, watching. They had come out in canoes, on bits of wood, clinging to anything that would float, just to see the visitors.

The Pacific islands may be remote, but all were settled long before the arrival of the Europeans, and without benefit of compass or sextant. The craft the settlers used were outrigger sailing canoes, or their heftier cousins, Polynesian double canoes.

How did these people navigate across such emptiness? Years ago, I decided to find out. A small island at a great distance presents the hardest target to hit, so it was no accident that Micronesia was where I discovered a few navigators still practicing traditional methods. There, experts like Hipour taught me basics: the "star path," different for each course and island; the complexities of steering by island sightings; the subtle patterns of ocean swells rebounding from topography dozens of miles distant; the particular clouds that form over islands below the horizon; the bird species that signal land no more than a day's flight away ... clues that add up, none utterly reliable

The gable of a ceremonial house, its bark facade painted with the stylized faces of protective spirits, pierces the sky above a village in Papua New Guinea. Many among the 700 linguistic groups here share a belief in spirits and sorcery— and a certain deference to the tourist industry. Villagers may now sell masks and carvings once used only for ceremonies. Western Samoan builders (right) still use coconut-fiber rope to lash a roof onto a fale, *one of their traditional open-air houses. Now nails add extra strength. Inside many* fales, *modern furniture clutters cool stone floors, where only mats once lay. Chairs and beds serve mainly as catchalls; no one sits or sleeps on them.*

At home on the water, a Badjao village of the southern Philippines rests on wooden stilts. Houses connected by catwalks shelter families who depend on coral-reefed lagoons for a living. There they hunt shark and other fish, for food and for trade. The Badjao are said to possess uncanny sailing skills: They can identify discrete points at sea by name or determine travel time by testing the currents with a finger. Today's technology has invaded even the afterlife. Miniature canoes often rested on Badjao graves, left there to carry the spirits of the departed; now the spirits get to ride in models of gasoline-powered outboards.

by itself, but dependable when weighed together by the wisdom of experience.

Pacific navigators had experience aplenty. Until Europeans fanned out over the globe, Polynesians were perhaps the most far-flung people on Earth. Where did they come from? Students of language history think Pacific sailing-canoe terms derive from 4,000-year-old Austronesian tongues.

That means the oceangoing canoe probably developed in the world's most populous island nation: Indonesia. The people of the 6,000 habitable islands of the East Indies have been sailing at least that long, to get from one island to the next. Distant trade was flourishing over 2,000 years ago. Indian traders infiltrated the archipelago, bringing Hinduism and Buddhism. From Indonesia's legendary Spice Islands, the Moluccas, cloves and nutmegs passed through chains of sailing entrepreneurs, ultimately to reach the markets of Rome.

In recent centuries, internal Indonesian trade has relied on the humble *prahu*. These sailing craft, of varying sizes and rigs, are operated by a kind of oceangoing peasantry—mainly the archipelago's Bugi, Makassarese, and Madurese peoples.

"Satu, dua, tiga—one, two, three," chant the crews as they haul up the heavy anchors and sweat up the great lateen sails. Over Sunda Kelapa, one of the old prahu ports serving Jakarta, a forest of masts rises—a sight long gone from Western commercial ports. Men heft heavy sacks of rice and gypsum along narrow gangplanks that have carried not only goods but also such cultural staples as language and religion.

In the interest of dubious and cosmetic "modernization," motorized vessels are squeezing the prahus out, but in the 1980s prahu crews were still operating some 3,000 sailing craft of 50 feet or more, not to mention countless smaller ships.

I sailed with the five-man crew of one prahu for a few days. From Tonduk, one of the tinier islands east of Java, we cast off to the rhythm of an ancient chant and the beating of the gongs that would ensure a successful venture. The crew was setting out for distant reefs to collect and smoke sea slugs—trepang—for the Chinese market.

So short of water and fuel is arid Tonduk

Barking the right tree: A baobab, of a species native only to Madagascar, supplies a Vezo man with the makings for rope (opposite). He first carves out large sections of bark and cuts them into strips, then lets them soften in water. Strong teeth and nimble fingers tightly twist the strands (left and above) into a fibrous cord that can be woven into rope or net. This baobab is one of countless plant and animal species unique to long-isolated islands—species that are possibly useful, often endangered, but mostly unknown.

111

that we had to fill the great wooden water tanks at another island two days later. Otherwise, apart from the sacks of rice on board, we were self supporting, relying on the fish we caught.

We were following a tradition recorded in the temples of Borobudur, in Java, where 1,100-year-old carvings include detailed depictions of trading ships—no mere coastal craft but substantial decked-in multimasted vessels, some balanced by massive outriggers, others beamy enough to do without. The Romans Strabo and Pliny saw vessels such as these, probably from Sumatra, in the Red Sea in the first century A.D.

For centuries, perhaps millennia, the stabilizing outrigger appears to have been the world's most widespread voyaging invention. By A.D. 1000, outrigger designs had helped settle the islands of not one ocean, but two. From the East Indies people spread island by island more than halfway around the globe. They reached Easter Island—farther east than California—at one extreme, and the great isle of Madagascar, across the Indian Ocean, at the other.

Imagine sighting Madagascar's eastern coast. Rising from a fringe of palms, rugged slopes wall off the horizon, dwindling out of sight to left and right. No isolated pile of cumulus here. Humid Indian Ocean winds rise against the mountain front, creating a long rank of misty white where the moist air releases rain on the slopes.

Madagascar is a mini-continent, a thousand miles long. Were its people not so fond of wandering, many could easily live out their lives in the interior without ever seeing the surrounding sea. Yet its presence affects their lives, even their speech.

Their island is Earth's fourth largest, after Borneo, in the East Indies. And despite the intervening 4,000 miles, both islands have related Malayo-Polynesian languages.

Which is remarkable, considering Madagascar lies only 250 miles from Africa.

Archaeological traces suggest Malayo-Indonesian peoples came to Madagascar, perhaps around A.D. 1000, from settlements they had established on the African coast. Apparently they brought some Africans with them, rather like the Norse bringing Celts. Malay blood dominates in today's

Malagasy people, and Malay customs mix with African, preserved by the ocean barrier. You can see it in the very houses: round on the nearby African mainland, but rectangular here, as in Indonesia. Among other Malay imports: coconut, breadfruit, yams, bananas, the xylophone, terraced agriculture—and the outrigger canoe.

European ships eventually eclipsed the outriggers, and their arrival changed islands everywhere, perhaps nowhere more than in the Caribbean. Unlike Pacific peoples, many of whom survived the new era, Caribbean natives almost vanished. Europeans and forcibly transplanted Africans resettled the islands. Thus the Caribbean has less unity of tradition than the Pacific.

Each Caribbean island follows to some extent the ways of the overseas country that owned or settled it, not necessarily those of the adjacent island. Move clockwise around the Caribbean from island to island and imported languages flicker by: Spanish in Cuba, English in Jamaica, then French, Spanish, English, Dutch, French, English, French, English, more French, more English, and in Curaçao, a Portuguese-Dutch-Spanish mix called Papiamento.

So culturally varied is the region that you could call the Caribbean an eighth continent. Unfortunately, it does not have the natural resources of a continent. But it does have the island-paradise lure, and that can present its own problems.

You could see one of them in the tiny branch office of a credit union in the Îles des Saintes, a miniscule archipelago off Guadeloupe. The office, which opened for only four hours a week, was jammed with tourists and Saintois. An angry American demanded in broken French to know why yet another local had been invited to cut in front of him. How could you change your money with this going on? An equally angry woman shot back in Saintois dialect. How could she pay her bills with all these foreigners clogging the only bank she had? That's why she gets served first!

Such strains occur on touristed islands everywhere. But tourism is one of the few

Archers of North Sentinel Island celebrate the effect of a few well-placed arrows: the repulsion of a boatload of visitors bearing gifts to their shore. The Sentinelese are one of four tribes scattered through the Andaman Islands, a chain of more than 200 islands in the Bay of Bengal. They are the only tribe in this Indian territory that still refuses contact with outsiders. They have no televisions or telephones—and no pneumonia, measles, syphilis, or influenza. But they do have the future to fear. Business interests seek to transform the Andamans into a Hong Kong-style free port, a prospect hard to stop with an arrow.

The electronic assault on island isolation shows itself in a Tongan family's Christmas display. Residents of this Polynesian kingdom often receive televisions and elaborate radios—status symbols here—from relatives working overseas. No television station has yet arrived in Tonga, but video recorders and satellite dishes have. Imported change is nothing new here; Tongans such as these enthusiastically practice the religion that missionaries brought two centuries ago.

114

ways small islands can fuel a cash economy. Their other resources are too limited. Volcanic or coral islands have virtually no metals, no coal, no oil.

Aside from tourism and the dubious option of offering military bases, small, strapped island nations have little but the sea for sustenance and cash. For that reason they must occasionally take on goliaths. In 1984 the Solomon Islands, dependent on copra and fishing, defended its 200-mile limit by arresting the crew of an American tuna boat. The United States backed down, but banned imports of Solomon tuna.

Iceland is not so small, but its terrain and climate leave it with fewer resources than islands half its size. Fish products account for three-quarters of exports. "If it weren't for the fishes," one Icelandic official has asserted, "this island would be uninhabitable." In naval confrontations in 1958 and 1972, Iceland fought—and won—two "cod wars" with British trawlers.

By 1982 the United Nations Law of the Sea Convention was giving island nations new clout: sovereignty over natural resources within 200 nautical miles of any coast—even that of the smallest atoll. In the island-pocked Pacific, the effect has been to create a kind of phantom economic continent, stretching from Japan almost to Chile.

Islanders have another kind of resource as well, one threatened by the modern world but rooted in the eons: their native flora and fauna. Many island worlds developed outside continental time. Isolated from waves of evolutionary change on the mainland, ancient species could survive on an island, and unique new ones appear. The distinctive birds and beasts of the Galápagos, for example—each adapted to the conditions of its particular island—helped lead Darwin to the theory of evolution.

In elegant parallel to human societies, such islands nurture and protect species unknown on the mainland, taking on scientific importance far greater than their size.

Economic importance, too. Only in the isolation of the Moluccas did nutmeg and clove trees evolve, sparking a competitive international trade that would help steer human history for 2,000 years.

In Madagascar, subject to the deforestation and overgrazing that plagues much of Africa, the stakes are especially high. When the island split off from the mainland about 80 million years ago, it took the plant and animal species of that time with it. From those Cretaceous ancestors came uncounted species that live only here. The oldest branch of the human family tree—the lemur—survives here. Displaced elsewhere by monkeys, 26 species of lemurs cling precariously to the last 20 percent of the island's original rain forest.

One species of baobab tree grows in Africa; Madagascar has six, also menaced. These bulbous trees, whose lifespan measures centuries, do not fruit every year, and when they do, the seedlings are vulnerable

to foraging cattle and goats, animals needed by the Malagasy people.

It is not the first time people have changed an island ecosystem. The Polynesians themselves drastically altered the islands they found, importing taro (a starchy tuber, traditional mainstay of their diet), yams, pigs—even the palm trees.

The Polynesian migrations were probably prompted by the same factor endangering island wildlife: swelling human populations. It is an old problem, getting worse. The prehistoric Marquesans, fleeing their drought-prone archipelago, could have been the original Easter Islanders. On many islands, fear of invasion by desperate outsiders (Continued on page 122)

A logjam of lighters crowds Singapore's old harbor (opposite); the boats service cargo ships anchored offshore. This booming island nation also boasts one of the world's most modern containerports. Singapore owes its standard of living —second in the Far East only to Japan—partly to its fine harbor, located at a junction of international trade routes. By contrast, Australia's remote Norfolk Island has no harbor at all. Here, importing even one of life's larger necessities presents difficulties (above).

117

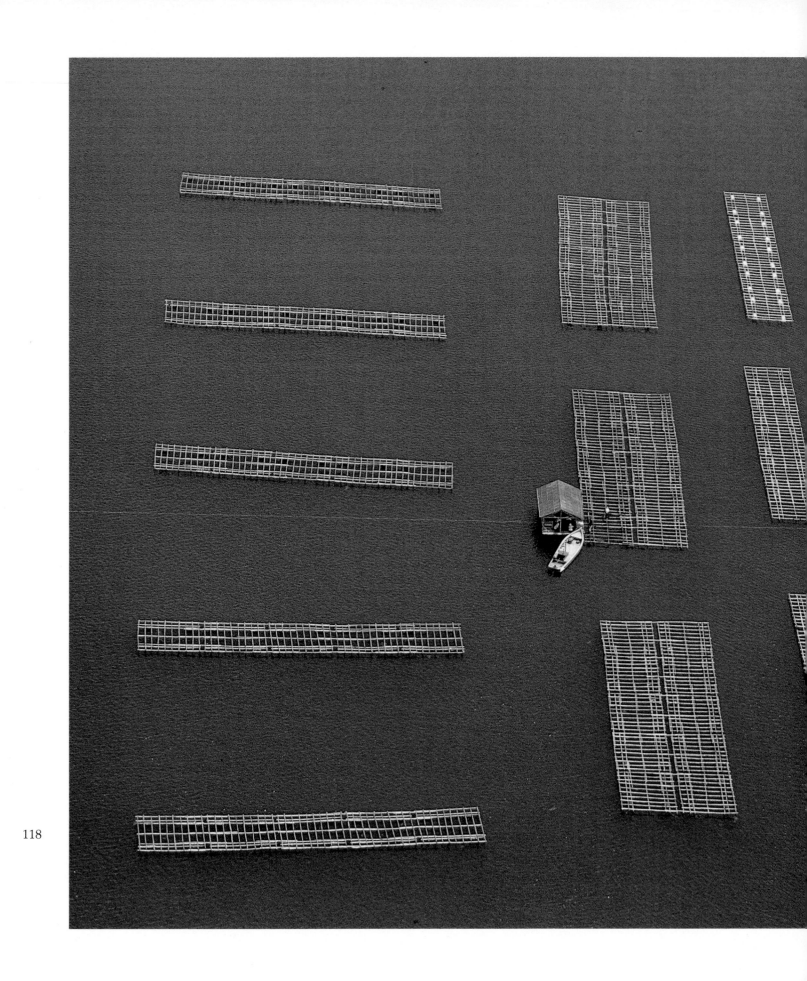

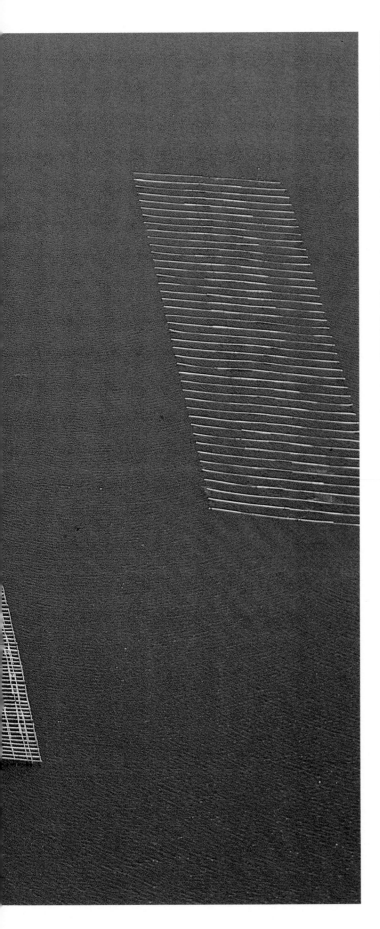

Buddhist temples reflect tranquil beauty on Japan's largest island, Honshu. Beauty of a smaller kind grows hidden in the pearl farms of Ago Bay (left). Under these bamboo rafts pearl oysters hang in wire baskets, each mollusk slowly coating a tiny implanted bead with nacre —mother-of-pearl.

NEXT PAGE: Divers inspect pearl oysters strung up in a French Polynesian lagoon. Pearl cultivation on strings is losing favor to baskets, which don't require drilling holes in the oystershells.

119

fostered an automatic xenophobia. Land was so precious in parts of Polynesia that it was often the custom to bash any castaway on the head. He could, after all, be a Tongan. Tongans today are peaceful, but their bellicose ancestors became notorious for taking over islands.

Now improved health care is triggering population crises. Fewer children die from diseases. Tahiti, the classic island paradise, has grown so crowded that Club Med sought isolation for one of its escapist resorts by siting it on nearby Moorea.

Overcrowding has led—sadly—to emigration. Although the cost of air and sea transport is high for remote islands, air travel has helped by opening up the out-

side world. Many islanders of today's Pacific now study or work abroad. Family ties remain strong. Thousands of Rarotongans now work in New Zealand, but most continue to send money to relatives back home.

Mid-ocean islanders are not the only ones with overpopulation problems. With almost three times the land area of Texas, Indonesia as a whole does not suffer from the limitations of small archipelagos, having a wealth of rice, coffee, sugar, rubber, spices, tin, bauxite, copper, and above all oil. But two-thirds of its population, some 100 million people, are crammed onto the 620-mile-long island of Java. That's 2,000 people per square mile. (The density in the U. S. is 67.) Java's scores of volcanoes

The sea's harvest comes hard in Alaska's Aleutian Islands. A tired crew unloads live snow crabs from the holding tank of the Aleutian Mariner, *a 118-foot vessel that exploits the bountiful Bering Sea. This trip's haul: 162,800 pounds, about average. Sometimes at sea for weeks at a time, the men work backbreaking 20-hour shifts bringing in crab pots (far left) by the hundreds. They get a break when hurricane-force winds, which can top 120 miles an hour, whip up high seas. Crabbing is one of the Aleutians' most lucrative industries, but for some Aleut natives, the traditional way of life—crabbing just for the day's meal—makes more sense.*

123

account for its rich soil and indirectly, perhaps, for its population crunch, as the fertile soil and hot moist climate can produce three rice harvests per year. Now, however, this is not enough to feed all the people.

A Javanese farmer told me about the government's solution, the policy of *transmigrasi*. His fields clung to the flank of a volcano, Mount Bromo, which happened to be erupting at the time. I had earlier looked into the inner crater, where thunderous bursts were hurling three-foot lava bombs into the air, and broke all records getting out of there. The farmer was not in danger, but the inferno raging inside his mountain somehow added urgency to what he said.

"I have three boys. How can I hope to leave them enough land to live on when these fields barely support us now? That is why we are going. We have put down our names for transmigrasi."

"Where will you migrate to?"

"Sumatra most likely. The climate and soil are said to be like that here, and there are empty spaces."

Indeed, a comparatively sparse 90 people to the square mile live on the California-size island of Sumatra. The transmigration program is voluntary, the farmer told me. I later confirmed his astonishing assertion that 2.5 million rural Javanese were to be transplanted during one five-year plan alone. The greater number will go to Sumatra, others to Borneo or the southeastern islands. And some will go to Irian Jaya—western New Guinea, as part of a controversial program of "Indonesianization." The New Guinea natives are Melanesian, and critics say the program smacks of Javanese cultural conquest—not unlike the West's cultural conquest of the Pacific.

That Pacific conquest continues. When islanders gave me a tour of Raiatea, French Polynesia, they included their taro-growing marsh—as a "historical site." Everyone now used flour from France. A typhoon of foreign ideas continues to wash over small island societies—borne by television, magazines, business people, and tourists.

Tourism, in a perverse way, also helps keep old customs alive. A kind of hula-and-pareu culture that I call "Film Tahitian" now pervades the Pacific. It is preservation, of a sort. And sometimes island ways encouragingly reassert themselves. I remember watching a Tongan teenager walk along the shore. She wore an American T-shirt and blue jeans, and was eating a raw fish.

High-rise housing developments (opposite) offer hope to the poor of Guadeloupe, a French department in the Caribbean. On such tropical islands the encircling sea may mean a luxury escape for mainlanders, but a poverty trap for locals. The twain meet on a rake-groomed Jamaican beach (above, left). Island governments thus face a dilemma. Their best economic hope—tourism—may spawn assembly-line hotels, accentuate the gap between rich and poor, and turn respected tradition into cheap sideshow. They struggle to solve the paradise paradox: How to prosper without destroying the very things that give islands their appeal, for visitor and native alike.

124

DAVID LEWIS

125

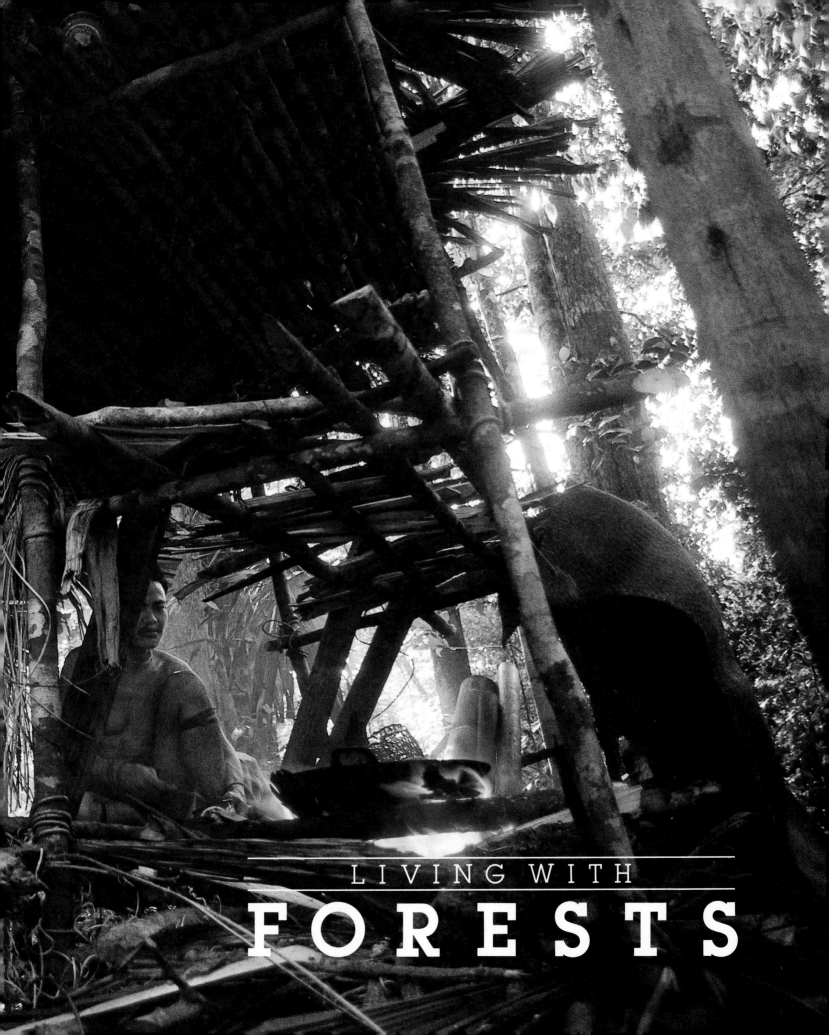

LIVING WITH
FORESTS

I was a hulking giant, a six-foot-two anthropologist among full-grown men and women barely four and a half feet tall. In my native Scotland, it's considered a good thing to be tall. But in the Ituri Forest of central Africa, the Mbuti—one of the peoples we call Pygmies—merely felt sorry for me.

I was too tall to slip through the underbrush. Too white to blend into the jungle shadows. Too heavy to stalk game without a great crackling of twigs and leaves underfoot. They said I sounded like an elephant. I even smelled funny; not until I'd shared their diet for several months did I begin to develop their characteristic smoky smell.

So I'd never make a hunter. But I'd do nicely as *mbavu*—a fool, a harmless scapegoat to blame things on. If one man cuckolded another, *I* was the culprit—and who could hold a poor fool accountable for his deeds? If we went hunting and bagged nothing, well, no wonder; *I* was along.

And so, during field research spanning three decades, I filled my niche as peacekeeper and safety valve among the Mbuti, a people marvelously attuned to life in a standing forest. Long ago my distant ancestors knew the ways and moods of the forests that blanketed most of Europe. Now those woodlands are all but wiped away by the cultures we, their descendants, have wrought. And now those cultures send researchers like me to study people who live in a forest without cutting it down.

There are few such people in the world today. Humans have had to cut down trees as part of the transition from hunting and gathering to farming. Forests once covered at least half of Earth's land area. Now they cover less than a third, and most of that is land too rocky or steep or dry or cold or remote for us to use for something else.

Often a forest is either a resource to be harvested, or it's in the way. We need the wood for lumber and fuel, or we need the land for a farm or highway. In this age of oil and atoms, half the world's people still depend on firewood—an energy source that is dwindling even as populations explode.

Forests are among nature's most complex ecosystems. Walk with the Mbuti among the trees, and you brush against plants in profusion—so many kinds that science has yet to describe them all. For this is tropical rain forest, one of three great stands—others are in Amazonia and Southeast Asia—that circle our world at its waist.

In these equatorial forests the sun never travels far to the north or south, so temperature varies little from season to season. Plants hold their leaves all year, and any season finds fruits and nuts ripening.

In some tropic areas the rains make the seasons. If you visit a forest here in the dry months, you may find it's not the lush, tangled jungle of the Tarzan movies. Brown leaves rustle overhead or crunch underfoot. But return when the rains do, and you will see new life budding and blooming as the forest drinks deep and blushes green.

Beyond the tropics, in lands where the seasons run hot and cold, stand the familiar pines and oaks and maples of the temperate deciduous forests—chiefly in the Northern Hemisphere, where most of the temperate land is. There are temperate rain forests too; in coastal areas where the sea keeps winters mild, broadleaf or needleleaf evergreens flourish.

Far north of the tropics stand the boreal forests called taiga, where hardy coniferous evergreens endure the short summers and bitter cold winters of lands approaching the Pole. In Siberia's semiarid fastnesses the deciduous larch rules the forest, shedding its needles in autumn and sprouting new ones in spring.

The farther you go from the Equator in this succession of forest types, the less richness you're likely to find in the variety of plants. A square mile of tropical rain forest may hold 300 species of trees, a temperate forest perhaps a tenth of that—and some expanses of taiga stretch away for mile after mile dominated by a single kind of conifer. Thus it is mainly in the warmer climates that humans find the varied resources needed for life in a forest.

Even so, the richest of forests can only feed a relatively small population. A single nomadic Mbuti band may muster about 100 people, usually less. Given such numbers, a large forest can easily supply most of their needs. In so doing, it becomes like a parent. And its soul is *ndura*, the life-force of the

Marooned in a sea of trees, a Lese village clings to a road in Zaire's Ituri Forest. In small clearings the Lese tend crops, slashing and burning a new plot each year. Fruits, meat, and materials for huts come mainly from forest-dwelling Mbuti Pygmies in return for vegetables and trade goods. For centuries this symbiosis has sustained both peoples with little impact on the forest—the exception, not the rule, as humans worldwide have cleared forests for farms and towns or to get lumber and firewood.

PREVIOUS PAGE: In the Sarawak rain forest on the island of Borneo, a Punan hunter and his family perch in their palm-thatched shelter on stilts.

Our Shrinking Forests

Trees mantle almost a third of Earth's land area, as shown in dark green on this map. But the light green shows that, if humans vanished and climate stayed the same, forests would cover twice the area they do today. Humans make the difference; we clear land for cultivation and harvest wood to build or burn. When our herds graze on cleared land, they destroy sprouts and keep the forest from growing back. Our pollutants do the same by killing trees or blocking their reproduction. Europe's forests *fell mostly in medieval times, America's in the three centuries after the Mayflower. Now tropical lands feel the effects—good and bad—of deforestation: farms for the landless and mines and exports to bolster economies, but at the risk of soil depletion and even worldwide climate change. Preservation and reforestation offer our only hope that humans may again walk among trees on lands once forested.*

▨ Potential for Natural Forest

▨ Existing Forest

Ocean

EUROPE

BLACK
FOREST

ASIA

S   I   B   E   R   I   A

HIMALAYAS

North

Pacific

Ocean

Philippines

AFRICA

ITURI
FOREST

Mambasa

SARAWAK
FOREST

Sumatra

Borneo

New
Guinea

Madagascar

Indian Ocean

AUSTRALIA

South

Atlantic

Ocean

New Zealand

forest that cradles and sustains the Mbuti.

"*Ema epa ndura,*" they sing to the forest as they gather honey or *eseli* nuts or edible fungi. "Mother father forestness." I point to a broken sapling, and they say "Ndura," for the life-force may yet send a new shoot from its roots. I pick up a fallen leaf and say "Ndura," but they correct me, for the life-force has left the leaf and will not return; it is part of the forest but not of the forestness.

Some Mbuti bands hunt with bow and arrow. But today I am among the net hunters. While the women gather mushrooms, nuts, and berries, the men and I set up the vine nets in a great arc that sweeps for half a mile or more. Then the women close in on the arc with all the fuss and racket they can

make. We are lucky; a duiker—a small forest antelope—darts into the net and thrashes until the owner of that section of net kills it with a spear.

Though they kill, the Mbuti tell me that killing offends the forest. That is why, before this hunt began, the children built a fire of leaves to announce the hunt to the forest. Whether for propitiation or for luck, each hunter had to pass through the smoke.

A generation ago, when this was the Belgian Congo, Belgian officials sought to turn the Mbuti into farmers. Along the road that bisects the Ituri, I watched an official lure some of them out of the forest and teach them to plant beans. But as soon as he went away, they dug up the beans and feasted on

Forests provide animals and the weapons to hunt them. An Mbuti in Zaire makes a bow by heating and bending a stick. Another aims an iron-tipped arrow made for antelope and other big game. When he hits his target, he pops the bow-string against the monkey skin on his wrist to tell other hunters to watch for the stricken animal. Smaller game calls for arrows tipped with poison extracted from a vine. In Borneo, a Punan hunter dips blowgun darts in poison (above) from ipoh *trees.*

133

them. Why wait six months for food to grow when it is all around every day?

The Mbuti are not alone in the forest. For centuries the Bira, Lese, and other Africans have carved out villages and gardens and lived in symbiosis with them. The Mbuti labor in the villagers' gardens and bring them the forest's bounty—honey, meat, and poles and thatch for mud-walled huts. The villagers supply the Mbuti with iron tools, cloth, produce, and in modern times the small sums of cash needed for medical care or the wares of the outside world.

It takes the villagers months to cut a clearing, but it will support crops for only a year before the soil plays out. Each year they clear a new site, until finally the gar-

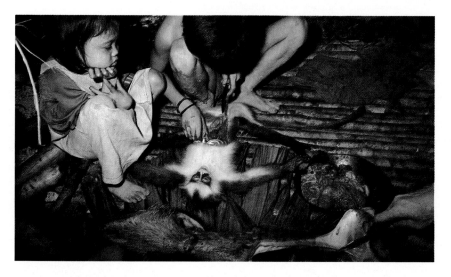

Forest dwellers find food in nature's larder. In Brazil's Amazon basin, Kayapo Indians roast a live tortoise in its shell. Sometimes the cook will hack open the tortoise's belly, scoop out the innards, and fill the cavity with manioc flour.

A Punan family on the island of Borneo gut a monkey and a wild pig (above). Building a diet around game and a starchy porridge made from the cores of sago palm stems, these people eat once a day—and never have to drink liquids, thanks to the palm's moisture.

dens are so far away that they must transplant the village. The forest is pocked with old clearings in various stages of recovery.

The secret of living in a forest lies in low numbers spread thin. Perhaps this helps to explain the Mbuti's horror tales—of demons called *Shetani*, of monsters whose long arms snake through the trees and grab a person unawares. In trumpeting his own bravery, the storyteller may also be encouraging the villagers to stay out of the forest. Now and then a leopard drags off a villager's goat as if to drive the lesson home.

Villager and Pygmy now face a challenge beyond the reach of scare stories. Other Africans are moving into the forest. Some seek lumber, coffee, rubber, game. Others

134

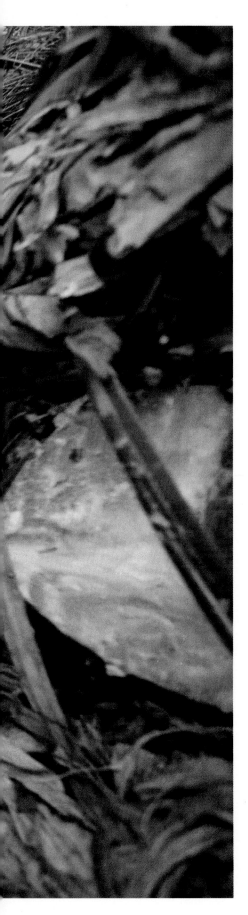

To make a palm wine called libondo, *a Zaire villager perches on a scaffold, cuts back the crown of a raffia palm, and drives funnels into the cut leaf bases to drain sap into a gourd. The gourd fills in about four hours. In this hot climate the sweet liquid begins to ferment as soon as it is drained from the tree.*

In an arid baobab forest in western Madagascar, a Mikea forager finds a bee tree, quiets the insects with smoke, then reaches in to take the honey and run. A Mikea girl samples the find right from the comb. Honey supplements a diet of sweet potatoes and babo roots, *vital reservoirs of moisture that allow the Mikea to survive in this nearly waterless forest.*

137

Like people in most tropical forests, farmers in Zaire clear land by the slash-and-burn method. Here men chop down trees and women set fire to the debris (above), leaving fields to smolder for days or even for weeks. The ashes release nutrients into the poor soil—a characteristic of tropical rain forests—but cultivation soon depletes the soil and new fields must be cleared. Tropical forests quickly reclaim small plots, but this large patch, stripped for a plantation in the Ituri, will recover much more slowly.

are farmers who cut great clearings for plantations. The villagers get by with a garden, for they live partly off the forest through their partners the Pygmies. But the ancient symbiosis of peoples like the Bira and Mbuti may vanish as the needs of the modern world and the allure of its material goods overtake the patterns of the past.

"When the forest dies," the Mbuti say, "we die." They could be speaking for forest cultures everywhere. As hunter-gatherers began farming, populations rose and trees fell for cropland to feed them. The life-style of the hunter-gatherer is all but extinct.

One of the few places it persists is in the most intricate ecosystem on Earth, the 2.7 million square *(Continued on page 148)*

Side-by-side with a kerchiefed villager, an Mbuti woman helps weed a village peanut patch (left, upper). The Mbuti often barter such labor for trade goods—palm oil, iron arrowheads, tobacco, salt—or a share of the crops.

By a villager's mud-walled hut, an Mbuti man pares a share of sweet potatoes with a machete (opposite). A steaming pot awaits the cleaned tubers.

Mbuti women (left) pound manioc leaves to make sombe, a staple of Pygmies and villagers throughout central Africa. They singe the leaves, pound them, boil them, then simmer the batch in palm oil to produce a mush resembling creamed spinach.

NEXT PAGE: Swinging on a liana, a Punan boy makes a jungle gym of Borneo's forest.

141

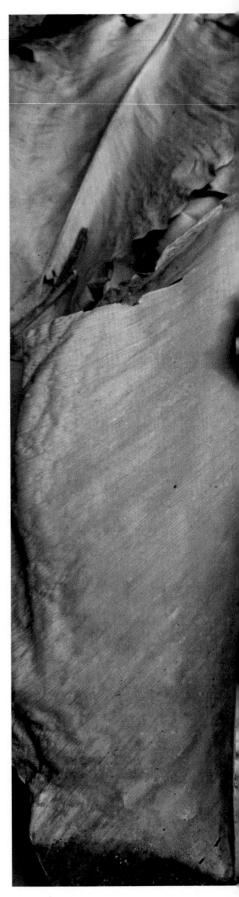

Materials gleaned from the forest put roofs over the heads of an Mbuti band in northeastern Zaire. To build a hut for her family, a woman jams a ring of saplings into the ground and entwines the tops. She then weaves some supple branches around the saplings, shaping a dome of lattice, and attaches mongongo *leaves by pinning them to the frame with their own stems bent double. Working up from the bottom, she laps the leaves like shingles to make the hut rainproof, then piles branches on top to hold* them in winds and downpours.

The entry usually faces the hut of friends or kin. But it may be relocated many times as relations between neighbors change. After a month or two the game has been depleted, the wild fruits and nuts have grown scarce, the honey has all been harvested. Then the whole camp—perhaps ten huts in a circle near a stream—moves on, rebuilding near a village or retreating into the forest. A social event—a death, a birth, a marriage, a puberty ceremony—will also trigger a move.

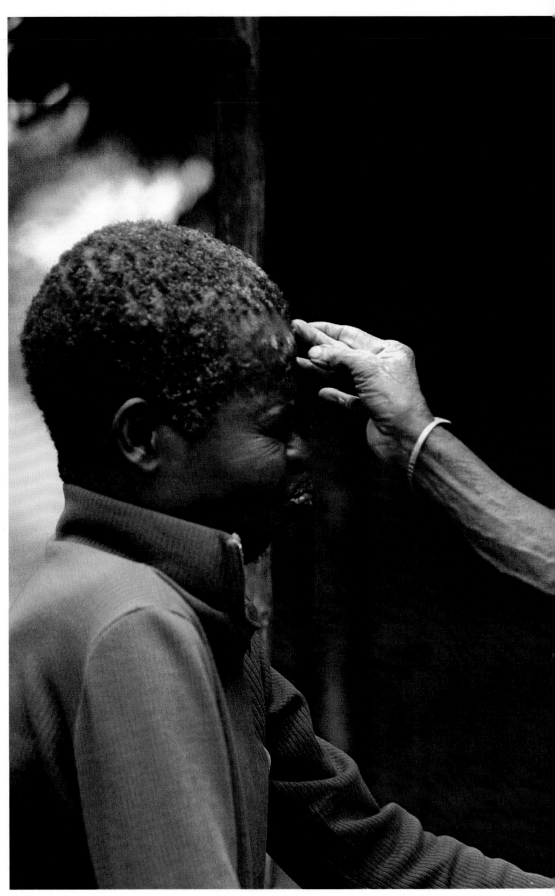

From the shelves of a forest pharmacy come treatments for human ills. To allay a villager's stubborn eye infection, an Mbuti woman (opposite) seeks out the proper plants for an herbal remedy. After charring selected leaves, she rubs the ashes into cuts she has made in the man's forehead.

The treatment did not cure the infection. Antibiotics might have—and many of these come from plants of the tropical forests. There, competition for light, space, and nutrients has forced plants to develop highly sophisticated chemical mechanisms. From tropical species, scientists have produced painkillers, birth control pills, and treatments for ills ranging from motion sickness to schizophrenia, cholera, and cancer.

147

miles of rain forest in South America's Amazon basin. Rain indeed rules here; between 80 and 160 inches of it soaks the forest each year. About half evaporates back into the air. At any moment 240 billion tons of moisture hovers in the clouds overhead.

Beneath those clouds stretches an undulating monotony of green—the canopy, roof of the forest, shingled with trillions of leaves as high as 150 feet above the ground. Little sunlight leaks through this ceiling, so the forest floor remains open, dark, and damp. But there is no monotony to the fabric of life: Nearly half the world's plant and animal species live here.

Humans have been part of this tapestry since at least 5000 B.C. Isolated tribes like the Yanomamö still live off the forest much as the Mbuti do—hunting birds, monkeys, and other game, harvesting wild fruits and nuts, and relishing a precious find of wild honey. Yanomamö men build curving lean-tos of poles and thatch, one joining the next until they close in a doughnut-shaped *shabono,* a communal home in which the tenants' only privacy is outside in the forest. In a year or two the insect pests take over—one roach species grows to more than three inches long—and the house is burned and rebuilt.

The Yanomamö and most other Amazonian tribes do their own farming. By slash-and-burn they clear a plot, then grow bananas, corn, and other crops until the weeds take over in two or three years and a new plot is cleared. Anchored to their fields and villages, such peoples lack mobility and have instead a strong sense of territory.

Fights erupt over land, water, fishing areas, even women. Brother may battle brother in a club fight over a woman—and afterwards wear a fearsome head scar as a badge of honor. But much of the warfare among villages is ritualized. The Yanomamö even invite enemies to their villages for feasts, taking care to spruce up the shabono, cook some plantain soup, and bedeck themselves with feathers and red pigment. The youths stage a ritual combat, egged on by the others. Such feasts can

forge alliances—or heat up to real fighting.

Though outside contact has altered tribal ways, the modern world has only nibbled at the fringes of this rain forest, the largest on Earth. Ranching, mining, logging, and farming eat away mostly at its eastern flanks, ravaging huge areas and arousing heated debate all over the world. Brazilian law tries to limit a developer to clearing half of any tract. Even so, Brazil clears an area the size of Connecticut every year. But so far, most of Amazonia—like the green mantle of central Africa—remains largely untouched by the hungers of the 20th century.

Not so the forests of southern Asia. Indonesia holds nearly a tenth of the world's tropical rain forest, but on Sumatra and Borneo it's falling to loggers and settlers. Malaysia has logged vast tracts for rubber and oil palm plantations. Only remnants survive in southern China and Indochina.

As you stand on the hot monsoon plains that cover much of India, you find it hard to believe that forests once robed the land around you. Now trees are so scarce that cow dung must be used as cooking fuel—a loss of badly needed fertilizer for deteriorating farmlands. Yet even in the hottest parts of India I have seldom failed to find, within walking distance, some cool, shady grove that is sacred and never cut, no matter how great the need for wood. Often I saw classes for children and adults being held in such a grove. I watched farmers detour on the way to or from work to stop and hear some holy man or simply to meditate in a remnant of the forest that once was.

New Guinea's forests have fared better, for they carpet a terrain too rugged for much logging. But in deep folds of peak and valley, isolated tribes that once farmed taro and sweet potatoes in forest clearings have begun to plant coffee instead. More will switch to this and other cash crops as new roads snake deeper into their highlands and link them with markets below.

Tropical rain forests took millennia to evolve. But a tract can be cleared in hours. The effects can last for centuries, for in most places the soil is surprisingly poor. Most nutrients are in the vegetation; strip it away and you leave little to nurture a crop.

Also, a forest is like a sponge, soaking

A road pierces the Ituri at its heart. To some forest people, it is like a poisoned arrow bringing death to the rain forest; to others, a welcome link to modern life. The one-lane highway opened the Ituri in the 1930s to Belgian and Greek settlers. Today it is an important truck route. Not far east of this undisturbed stretch of forest near Mambasa, coffee plantations straddle the road, some consuming 2,000 acres of the Ituri. The villages and Pygmy camps supply some plantation workers but not enough, so newcomers invade daily. Every acre cleared for plantations means seven more for workers' gardens and settlements. Each day the people of the Ituri look less to the forest for their needs.

Roads bring new goods to the forest. From Mambasa come bright fabrics, a machine to turn them into clothes (opposite), and a young woman to carry both home. Roads also bring new ideas. At a Catholic mission run by Italian priests, Mbuti and their village neighbors parade to church on Palm Sunday. Converts often enrich their Christianity with traditional beliefs and enjoy the new music and rituals along with their own. Missionaries have also brought medical care and Western education.

150

up downpours and releasing the waters slowly into steadily flowing streams. Forests not only hold the soil, they create it as fallen leaves and trunks decay into rich humus. Stripped of the forest, the soil erodes quickly, leaving the land impoverished.

Sometimes all it takes to change a forest is a road that lets in the sun. The road heats up, and so does land cleared along the roadside. I suspect that may help to dry out the roadside, which would kill more trees and create more open land to heat up. Whatever the causes, along some roadsides in both the Amazon basin and the Ituri, the forest has receded so far that you can't see it from the road.

But in tropical rain forests all over the

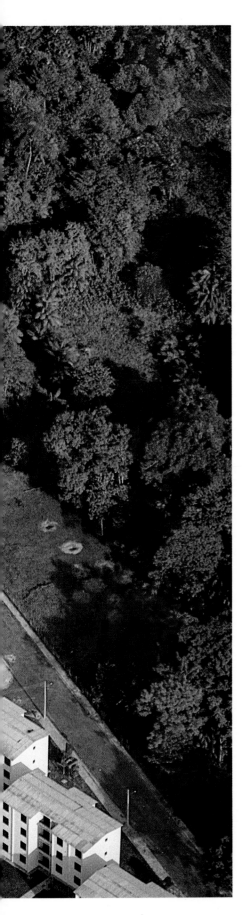

world you can see the logging trucks. Builders want the exotic woods—teak, mahogany, ebony. And Japan's fast-food outlets want throwaway chopsticks; America's want cheap beef. So down come the trees to feed the sawmills and create cropland and pasture. Worldwide, some 50 acres are wiped out in the time it takes you to watch a commercial for burger, fries, and shake.

Not even the scientists can tell us what we are losing, for millions of species yet undiscovered live in those forests. From the rosy periwinkle came medicine that can send leukemia into remission. From other plants come waxes, oils, dyes, and rubber; bananas, cashews, coffee, and quinine; ingredients for everything from drugs to deodorants to dynamite. About a fourth of the world's pharmaceuticals owe their origin to tropical rain forest. What might we discover tomorrow: a pest-resistant fruit? A cure for arthritis? An ark of unknown plants and animals? We may never get to find out.

Throughout the history of Western civilization, a forest has often been seen not only as a source of good cropland but as a place of darkness, a haunt of ghosts and demons. I remember being scared out of my wits by an old storyteller in Germany's Black Forest years ago. My intellect told me his vampires and werewolves were only fables, like the scare stories of the Mbuti. But I wondered whether they once had the same purpose: to encourage outsiders to stay outside.

If so, the stories didn't work. Europe's forests are but remnants, the leftovers from medieval farming, lumbering, shipbuilding, and fuel gathering. Only in the high latitudes have great expanses of forest survived, in a broad swath cloaking the northlands of Europe, Asia, and North America. This is the taiga, a Russian name, a reminder of the limitless miles of Siberian conifers so far from roads and sawmills and so stunted by cold and wind and a paucity of rain that men have not wanted either their wood or the ground they cover.

What is left of Europe's forests now seem wedged between phalanxes of conservationists and the engines of industry. In West Germany, politicians can rise or fall on the stand they take regarding *waldsterben*, the tragic "forest death" that is snuffing out the

On land gouged from the jungle near Belém, Brazil, blocks of buildings house apartment dwellers lured to the banks of the Amazon by development. The rush to exploit the rain forest—fueled by poverty and overcrowding elsewhere and the lure of minerals, timber, and land—imperils not only the forest but its peoples. In 1987 a pipeline in Ecuador (above) was hit by earthquakes and mudslides. Nearly 25 miles of it were wrecked, spilling out 100,000 barrels of oil that ruined rivers fished by Indians.

153

Brazilian rubber trees now prosper in the Far East, source of 85 percent of the world's natural rubber. A plantation worker in Sumatra scores a rubber tree (opposite), cutting half an inch deep to tap the inner bark. This starts latex dripping into a cup—perhaps two ounces of the milky liquid in an hour or two. In one day he and his son tap 375 trees.

Women on a Malaysian island (left) convert latex into rubber. Mixed with water and a mild acid, the latex coagulates overnight in shallow pans. The women then wash the spongy slabs in water, squeeze them with a hand-cranked wringer, and hang the sheets of rubber to dry.

155

156

Black Forest, storied home of gnome and stag and clockmaker. Men do make clocks here, but they also burn coal in factories and power plants. The sulfurous smoke taints air and rain. Trees that don't die from the toxins fall easy prey to bark beetles, disease, and other invaders.

Change is in the wind. In Europe, and all over the globe, laws and treaties mandate a cleanup and technology works out ways to do it. But change is slow and costly. Forests are still thinning out as some industries throw untreated wastes to the winds. Bohemia's forests may be the most pollution damaged in the world. Foresters in Czechoslovakia tend rows of seedlings in hopes of developing new strains that can shrug off the human impact. Americans and Canadians argue over the acid rain that kills fish and threatens trees in the northeastern portion of North America. Trees take a long time to grow—and a short time to die.

When the *Mayflower* fetched New England in 1620, its optimistic passengers crowded ashore to what seemed a fecund Eden of open, parklike forests and teeming fish and game. How, they wondered, could the local Wampanoag Indians live in poverty worse than the beggars of London amid such bounty? But by the end of the first winter, half the colonists had died, killed or weakened by hunger. In spring the Wampanoag came out of the forest, the men to launch heavy dugouts and fish offshore, the women and children to gather shellfish and crabs at the water's edge.

The colonists clung to an English dream: plant a farm, build a house, sink roots, stay put. But the Indians, seemingly poor because they owned no more than they could carry, lived off the land in tune with the seasons by moving to where the food was.

They too farmed in the summer, hoeing their fields with clamshells on wooden handles, then planting hills of corn and filling the spaces between with squash and beans. But with the harvest in—and some of it cached in pits lined with mats woven of reed—the Wampanoag villages vanished. Family wigwams of poles covered with mats or bark were dismantled in a few hours. Lugging mats, bows, fishing gear, some smoked meat, and whatever corn and

other produce they could manage, the Indians disappeared into the woods.

Through the fall they hunted deer and bear, roving in small groups over wide areas. When the snows flew, they regrouped in sheltered valleys to set up multifamily longhouses for a winter of fishing and hunting—and often of hunger stoically endured as part of the seasonal cycle. In spring, the Wampanoag were back at their fields, wondering why the colonists had starved in their first winter even as the colonists wondered why the Indians would go hungry instead of storing more of summer's bounty.

Sometimes the forest was in the way for even these woodland Indians. Kindling set ablaze around some tree trunks would kill

Felled by a chain saw, a venerable Alaskan spruce topples. Nationwide, debris left by loggers helps fuel fires that blacken up to four million acres a year. To contain a fire in Montana's Helena National Forest, a crew sets backfires (above) to burn the tinder ahead of a blaze. Some ground fires act as nature's housekeepers by clearing debris from the forest floor.

NEXT PAGE: To keep a fire road open, a crew torches roadside brush in California's Angeles National Forest.

157

the trees and let in the sun for crops. Once or twice a year the Indians set ground fires that swept the undergrowth from the forest without killing the big trees, thus making hunting and traveling easier. Now and then they burned off trees and all to create meadows and increase the game supply.

Gradually this patchwork of forests fell before the tide of colonists in need of farmland and traders in need of lumber for the builders and shipwrights of England, a land once forested from shore to shore but long since shorn of its woodlands. By the time the tide lapped at the Pacific Northwest and the Canadian north woods, loggers were felling the softwood evergreens not only for lumber but for paper pulp.

Native cultures faded with the forests. Descendants of the Wampanoag try to keep the ancient ways alive at Plimoth Plantation, an evocation of the life-styles of both Indian and colonist. But in much that once was woodland, both the forest and its people are only a memory.

In the 1950s I worked for a while in the gold mines of Yellowknife, a town in Canada's Northwest Territories. There I met Yellowknife Indians who still lived in tents, trapped fox and beaver, fished, hunted caribou, and gathered berries. They talked almost with reverence for their land, a patchwork of forest and open scrub, and they looked askance at those who exploited it. Well they might; I used to pick wild strawberries with them—and learned from them to blow off the arsenic-laden dust from the smoke of the mine.

One evening a Yellowknife Indian took me into the woods to spend a night with his family in their summer camp. Their large tent was pitched among the evergreens. For me it was an unusual night. More than a dozen of us were crammed into that tepee, with our feet in the center by the ridgepole, covered with heavy furs and skins against the cool of night. All night long, it seemed, men and women chattered away, sometimes seriously, sometimes laughing and joking, in a language I did not understand. But I did understand why my friend had brought me to this place—to see something of a life that had once been his.

Even the prospectors with whom I flew

A grapple loader hoists timber in a privately owned tract of forest land in Alaska (left). In nearby Tongass National Forest, loggers have clearcut thousands of acres of spruce and hemlock for pulp used in making rayon and cellophane.

A sawyer at a lumber mill in Washington State (above) drives a log through close-set parallel saws. From a computerized booth he jockeys the waiting logs into position, then adjusts, stops, or reverses the saws to get the most lumber from each log.

in floatplanes knew that the empty land they probed wasn't a wasteland. Sometimes we would be prospecting for gold where Indians long ago had camped while hunting caribou. And we knew that, if we found gold, here too might arise another impersonal concrete jungle. Trees would fall to make room for it, taking with them another bit of an ancient way of life.

The prospectors returned to the mines and submitted their reports—but one day they too would be back, bringing their families, in canoes and on foot, to a site shared by other humans in other times as a campsite. There they would spend a weekend or so in harmony with the forest, almost as if they too, like the Mbuti, were stepping through the smoke in propitiation for an offense against the forestness.

Until this century, it seemed that Americans had little thought for the future of their once sprawling forests. Then in 1905 President Theodore Roosevelt created the U. S. Forest Service. Conservation had taken on a new definition. No longer did it mean reserving tracts of forest until the loggers could get to them. Forests were recognized as a renewable resource, not to be leveled and left, but to be replanted. Forest parklands, carefully managed natural woodlands, and tree farms like the pulpwood plantations of the South stand today where great stumps once studded the landscape.

Today we ride elevators to glassy condos that rise where forests once stood. But we remember those forests in countless ways. Our streets are planted with trees and punctuated with parks that evoke the forests they replace. Our fireplaces echo the woodland campfires of our distant forebears, and over them hang paintings of wooded lakes and streams. Our attics hold camping gear until our next weekend in a shady campground. Our national parks and forests and refuges brim with campers, hikers, and tour buses. And who has not watched as a bulldozer leveled a patch of woods—and then found the site a year later full of houses with carefully planted trees in a subdivision named Woodland Shadows or Enchanted Forest? Much of our woodlands are gone, but we, like the Mbuti, are still passing through the smoke.

COLIN M. TURNBULL

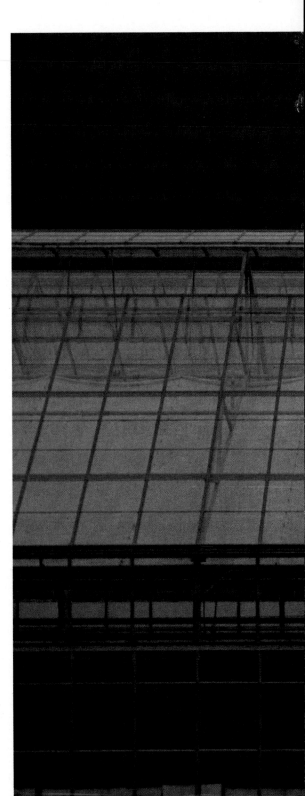

Science helps restore denuded forest land. This modern greenhouse in British Columbia sprouts 10 million seedlings a year for planting by the packful (above, lower) in parts of the 4 million acres in the province that await reforestation. In a laboratory near Seattle, Douglas fir clones take root in test tubes (above, upper). Seeking to develop superior trees, scientists created the clones by grafting the tips of branches from outstanding specimens of mature trees onto the growing root stock of other trees.

LIVING ON
GRASSLANDS

Our human origins are hazy and disputed, and there is much about our beginnings that we will never know, but two things seem fairly clear: that we started out somewhere in Africa and our Garden of Eden on that continent was a sunny, open landscape with more grass than trees.

Heavy forest impedes travel; open country inspires it. From Africa's grasslands, our ancestors diffused northward to the Mediterranean Sea and into the Middle East. Sooner or later, people spread outward to occupy every major grassland in the world. In time, they gave those grasslands many names. The great belts of shortgrasses that stretch across Eurasia would be called steppes; in North America, similar grasslands would be known as shortgrass prairies. The tall, lush grasses prevailing in temperate climates would be tallgrass prairies in North America, pampa in Argentina and Uruguay, and the veld in South Africa. Enough rain falls in these tallgrass regions to support trees, but periodic dry-season fires suppress woodland growth. Grasslands such as those in equatorial Africa and South America, with sufficient rain for trees but not enough to sustain forests, would be collectively known as savanna.

Each of these grassland biomes is habitable, and each has left a characteristic stamp on its people. But I've known grasslanders all my life, and I believe that grasslanders of different times and places share common traits. Some are exuberant and free, as if they hyperventilate from all that sky and wind. Some are restless, especially when they're on horseback, which has often been the case. Consider some stereotypes: Gauchos of the Argentine pampa and Cossacks of The Steppes, the Indians of the Great Plains, Texas drovers at full gallop down Front Street in Dodge City, wild-horse hunters and stockmen from Australian outback stations swaggering into Alice Springs in search of beer and entertainment, wild Mongol cavalries sweeping down upon Christendom from trackless steppes. Grasslanders all. A rich, colorful, and noisy company. Where would our legends and songs be without them?

Stereotypes, of course. And like their grasslands, few exist today in their natural state. Still, some of the best dreams die hard, and something of the old pride and freedom lingers.

Take the Masai of the East African savannas. Classic pastoral grasslanders, herders of cattle, the Masai are a statuesque people well nourished on their traditional diet of cow's milk mixed with blood drawn by arrow tip from the jugulars of cattle. They have never depended on hunting for food, but maintain a warrior caste, the *morani,* to protect their villages and herds and see to tasks that range from retrieving a strayed cow to subduing a wild rhino or, on occasion, killing a lion. Visitors to Masailand marvel at the tall young morani, standing storklike on one leg for hours as they watch over the precious herds.

"God gave us cattle and grass," the Masai say. "Without grass there are no cattle, and without cattle there are no Masai." Nomads for thousands of years, the Masai pursue a seasonal round in search of water and pasture for their herds. During the rains, when streams overflow and the grasses grow shoulder-high, they spread over the open plains and rolling foothills of the Great Rift Valley, settling in temporary kraals—mud-and-dung huts encircled by fences of thorn. The wet season is a time of little work, of singing, feasting, and initiation ceremonies.

With the arrival of the dry season, the land turns brown and water holes disappear. Many families leave their kraals and move their cattle to dry-season grazing in the highlands.

The Masai have generally resisted government edicts to modernize, clinging to their old traditions and mores. After the close of British colonial rule in the 1960s, when the new Kenyan government directed the Masai to adopt neo-African styles and settle in towns, they steadfastly refused. Today, many still dress their hair in the old ways and wear body paint, bangles, and togas. Many still roam East Africa's savannas.

Another nomadic grassland people, the Gidjingali of Australia's northern coastal savanna, once accepted a government plan to modernize—and then rejected it. Aboriginal hunter-gatherers, the Gidjingali moved

Neatly patterned windrows mark the efforts of an Alberta farmer at harvesttime on the Canadian prairie. For thousands of years, grasslands around the world have provided mankind with a major source of food: cereal crops. Hard work and improved technology have made Canadian grainfields some of Earth's most productive.

PREVIOUS PAGE: Admiring the fruits of his labor, a farmer stands amid a field of barley in Nebraska. Most modern farmers plant only one type of crop per field. This practice, known as monoculture, makes harvesting more efficient but exhausts soil and leaves it vulnerable to erosion.

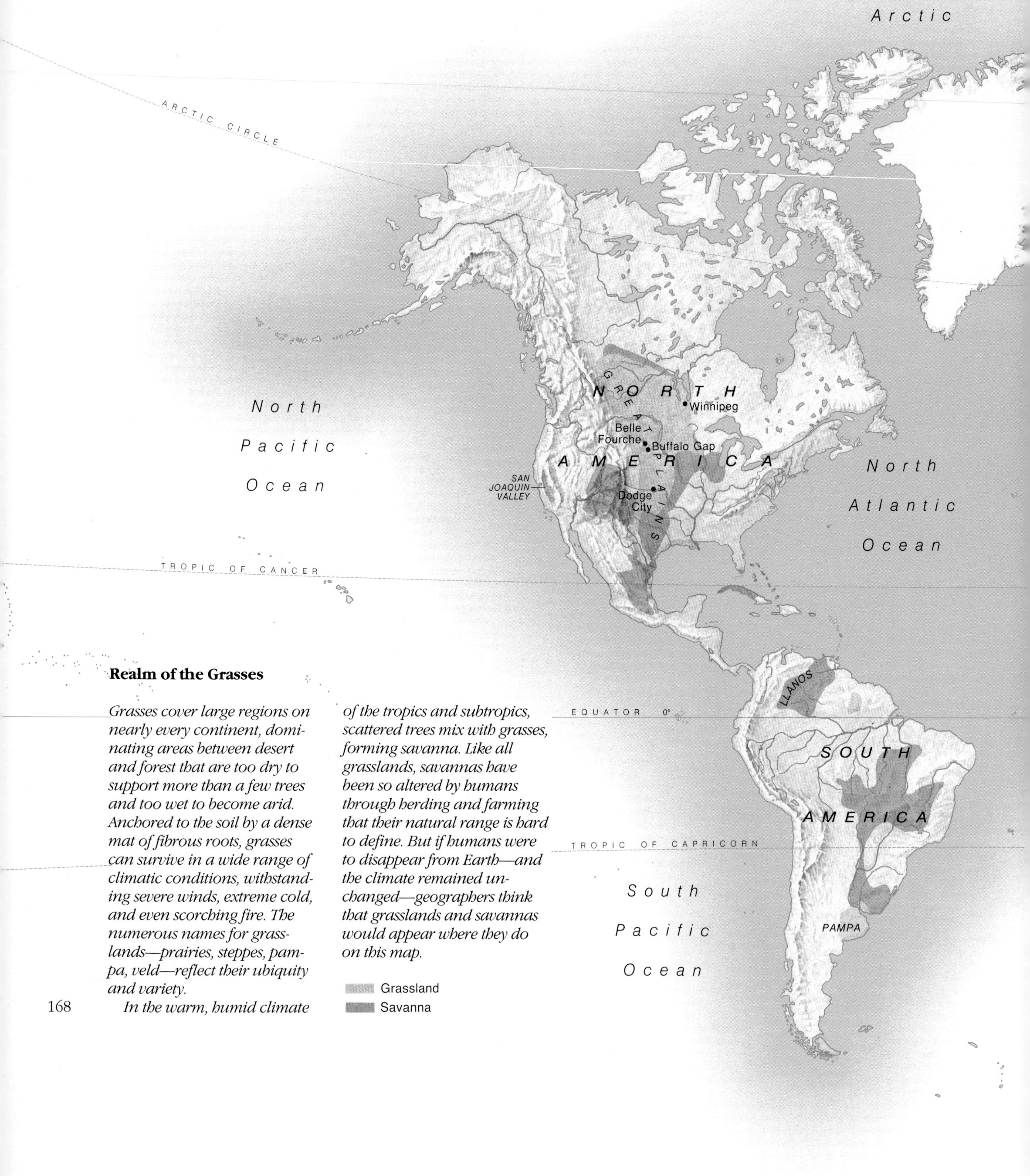

Arctic

ARCTIC CIRCLE

North

Pacific

Ocean

NORTH

• Winnipeg

Belle
Fourche •
• Buffalo Gap

GREAT PLAINS

SAN
JOAQUIN
VALLEY

AMERICA

Dodge
City

North

Atlantic

Ocean

TROPIC OF CANCER

Realm of the Grasses

Grasses cover large regions on
nearly every continent, domi-
nating areas between desert
and forest that are too dry to
support more than a few trees
and too wet to become arid.
Anchored to the soil by a dense
mat of fibrous roots, grasses
can survive in a wide range of
climatic conditions, withstand-
ing severe winds, extreme cold,
and even scorching fire. The
numerous names for grass-
lands—prairies, steppes, pampa, veld—reflect their ubiquity
and variety.
      In the warm, humid climate

of the tropics and subtropics,
scattered trees mix with grasses,
forming savanna. Like all
grasslands, savannas have
been so altered by humans
through herding and farming
that their natural range is hard
to define. But if humans were
to disappear from Earth—and
the climate remained un-
changed—geographers think
that grasslands and savannas
would appear where they do
on this map.

EQUATOR   0°

LLANOS

SOUTH

AMERICA

TROPIC OF CAPRICORN

South

Pacific

Ocean

PAMPA

168

Grassland

Savanna

Ocean

ASIA

EUROPE
Kiev

THE STEPPES

North
Pacific
Ocean

Mediterranean Sea

AFRICA

GREAT RIFT VALLEY

Indian Ocean

South
Atlantic
Ocean

VELD

AUSTRALIA

In a battle of wills, a Nuer herdsman in Sudan attempts to draw a calf from its cohorts. Nuerland and other parts of Africa's savanna receive too little rain to support regular crops, so local tribes turn to herding for their livelihood.

A hardy and adaptable species of humped cattle supply the Nuer with milk and meat, with hides for bedding, horns for utensils, dung for fuel. Cattle play a role in all Nuer ceremonies, in all Nuer social and economic exchanges. Like other pastoralists, the Nuer move with the seasons to support their herds. In the wet winters, when grass blankets the land and rivers flood, they congregate in villages of thatched huts built on high ridges. With the advent of the dry season, they disperse to riverside camps.

to government-established settlements in 1957. Fifteen years later, more than a third of the tribe's members left to return to their ancestors' lands and traditional ways.

Today, as in the past, the cycle of seasons governs the lives of these Gidjingali. In the wet season, they often locate their camps on an open spit near a river mouth or on dry dunes that penetrate the flooded swamps and plains. Here, where the sand is soft, the view wide ranging, and food readily available, they build their huts from the bark of eucalyptus trees. Men fish the rivers and stalk wallabies in the new growth of grass. Women forage for fruits and yams and catch plump rats by trapping them in a circle of fire.

As the dry season takes hold, members of the tribe congregate in large camps near the few remaining water holes and forage over the wide plains, digging for roots. To flush out game, they systematically burn off the bushland's dense undergrowth, touching firebrands to the dry grass and filling the sky with thick black smoke.

Later, just as the sweet berries of the *wombadjarr* ripen, storm clouds mass on the northern horizon, promising the relief of rain and the return to wet-season rituals.

hether in the savannas of Africa or northern Australia, the North American prairies or Argentine pampa, the world's early grasslanders adjusted well to life in the open. The Masai and the Zulu herded cattle, sheep, and goats, and built huts of mud and grass thatch; the pampa and llanos Indians, hunters and fishermen of South America, often built shelters of grass on frames of light poles; North American Indians roamed the Great Plains as hunters, moving their warm and easily portable hide tepees from camp to camp in pursuit of buffalo.

European newcomers, on the other hand, found open grasslands a shock. These pioneers were, almost invariably, the products of a culture whose patterns had developed with fields carved out of forest. In this new land, a horseman might ride for days without seeing a tree. And a farmer

171

confronted with the tough, dense sod of the prairie soon realized why the natives had usually been hunters first, and farmers a long second. It was a wrenching change, fraught with the difficulties that arise when a heritage is carried from the soil of an old culture into new landscapes.

On the American prairies, pioneers sought land with wood and water whenever they could. But as settlement proceeded outward from North America's woodlands, many made their homes in the remote outer reaches of the tallgrass prairies. With little wood for building, families constructed houses from sod—for most, an undesirable solution. They used twisted prairie grass for fuel. Buffalo chips burned well, too, but most pioneer women didn't relish the idea of cooking over manure.

These early pioneer farmers of the American Midwest quickly found that the plows they had used in the light forest soils of Europe and the eastern United States were almost useless in tallgrass prairies. The traditional plow, with its wooden or cast-iron moldboard to lift and turn the soil, simply didn't work: The moldboard failed to cut through the thick, fibrous sod. It wasn't until after the 1830s, when the thin, highly polished steel moldboard was invented, that a real prairie plow appeared and the conquest of the first met American grasslands began in earnest.

Most European comers to the grasslands—pioneers, gauchos, South African veld trekkers—shared a vein of cross-grained individualism. For one thing, each breed of settler included mavericks, people unwilling to fit in with established institutions back home (or perhaps even expelled by those institutions) and seeking to establish new ones. But whether honest folk or scoundrels, bond servants or convicts, adventurers or just plain people seeking the chance to get and keep land, the typical grassland settler was one who had turned his back on his old world and plunged into a new one.

In this new world, settlers often established homesteads miles apart from one another—unlike the natives they displaced, who usually banded together in communities or tribal units of some sort, living at close quarters. The latter, Australian Aborigines, North American Indians, Masai, had no real sense of individual ownership of land, and thus felt no need to divide that land into individual plots. Europeans, on the other hand, tended to claim large tracts of grassland as their own, each family of farmers settling in the center of sheer, grassy space. This self-imposed isolation often produced a measure of loneliness and an enhanced appreciation of human company—a quality that seems to persist today.

Growing up in a central Iowa town, I could sense this on Saturday evenings, especially in summer. Saturday was going-to-town day, when farming families cleaned up and came in for groceries and perhaps a haircut, and a chance to see the latest Tom Mix Western at the Twin Star. But mostly it was a chance to see friends and neighbors. Many of those people, I am sure, had spoken to no one but their family members for a week or more, and Saturday evening meant catching up, making up for lost time, trading news and gossip, seeing lights and hearing laughter and eating Blind Billy's peanuts and popcorn. The more isolated the settler, of course, the more valued such intercourse was likely to be.

One day not too long ago, big-game biologist Fred Priewert and I were making a pronghorn antelope survey in the Owl Creek prairie range northwest of Belle Fourche, South Dakota, when Fred stopped his pickup at a little road that led far off into the treeless grassland.

"A wonderful old gal lives down there a couple of miles," he said. "Widow woman. She runs this big spread with only two hired hands. Even breaks some of her own horses. One time when I dropped in on her with another biologist, she sat us down and told us we were going to get some of her pie and coffee. Seeing as how we had a few minutes to spare, I said, 'Why not?'

"Well, we drank about a gallon of black coffee while she made this apple pie from scratch, crust and all. When it was finished, she insisted that we stay and eat the whole thing. She wanted every bit of news about

"May God give you children and cattle." The two are rarely far apart in the prayers of the Masai, a pastoral tribe living in the grassy contours of East Africa's Great Rift Valley. For children, one must have cattle to provide milk, the main staple of the Masai diet. For cattle, one must have children to help with herding and husbandry.

A Masai woman collects cow milk in a calabash made from a dried and hollowed gourd (opposite). Amidst a swarm of flies, a child finishes the last milk from his mother's gourd.

173

what had happened since the last time she went to town, probably a month or six weeks before. It turned into a three-hour visit. Then she asked us to stay for supper!"

Similar stories are told, I'm sure, of remote stations in the Australian outback, distant farms in the Transvaal, and outlying *estancias* in the far reaches of the pampa. Congenial strangers are always welcome in such places. Shortwave radio and the airplane have helped shrink the immensities of the Australian outback, just as television satellites and dish antennas have brought much of the outside world to remote western ranches—but such things can never entirely supplant genuine human contact.

For any farmer or rancher, a trip to town

Masai youths, newly confirmed as warriors, file out at the end of a ceremony celebrating their status. "Young are the warriors, and we feed them the best of our meat," sing the senior warriors to the junior.

The Masai seldom eat meat —and never the meat of wild game, except during famine. But on special occasions, such as this Embolata Olkiteng *ceremony, they ritually slaughter and consume a bullock.*

For a Murle hunter (right), the wild white-eared kob is fair game. Seminomadic herdsmen of southern Sudan, the Murle are also skilled hunters. After the rains, when great herds of antelope and gazelles migrate through their lands, meat is abundant. Much of it they dry and keep for later use.

Mothers of Masai warriors construct a sacred hut from branches, leaves, and cow dung for a ceremony celebrating the promotion of senior warriors to elders.

Among the Masai, the building of houses as well as ceremonial huts is the business of women. To frame the traditional loaf-shaped hut, a Masai woman weaves together long branches, then patches the open spaces with grass and leaves—often from the leleshwa *bush*, which termites find unappetizing. Finally, she smears the walls and roof with a thick layer of cow dung to keep the hut warm and dry during the rainy season.

177

Without preliminary sketches, an Ndebele woman paints a bold geometric design on a prefabricated market stall in KwaNdebele, a semidesert "homeland" of 255,000 acres in South Africa's northern veld. Most Ndebele once lived and worked on their own arable land or on white-owned farms, such as the Onverwacht farm (right, upper). Under apartheid, they were forced to resettle in KwaNdebele. Traditional Ndebele homes—round huts with thatched roofs, mud-and-dung floors, and brilliantly painted walls—are rare in KwaNdebele. Cinder blocks and corrugated metal have replaced traditional building materials, which are scarce there.

or an occasional visitor can be a welcome break from the endless round of farming—growing food, raising livestock, caring for the land. From long before dawn to after dusk, it's plowing, planting, haymaking, walking the beans with hoe in hand. On the ranch, it's rounding up and feeding; branding in the spring. Up at all hours, chasing down the loose bull that wanders among the crops or minding a calf's midnight birth, arm shoulder deep in cow. Then the small chores neglected in the rush—the collapsed roof on the cattle shed, the downed fence wire far out in the field.

At planting and harvest times on any big farm, day often runs into night amidst the roar of machinery and the smell of diesel as tractors and combines big as cottages comb the land, lights blazing.

Most farmers on today's large farms—whether in North or South America, Australia, or South Africa—operate with a hefty complement of powerful equipment: combines, cultivators, tractors, grain trucks, sprayers, fertilizer and manure spreaders. But on ranches all over the world, one traditional grassland institution prevails and is likely to hold on for years to come: the horse. A horseless, dismounted life would

be unthinkable to many Australian stockmen and Asian steppe dwellers. On some of the big estancias of Argentina, gauchos and their *patróns* spend much of their working lives in their sheepskin saddles.

Even in our American West, the horse still has its place. (I have been told that "if God had meant man to walk, He'd have given him four laigs.") Pickup trucks have displaced horses for many jobs, but not all.

I was sharing a gas pump in the Buffalo Gap country of southwestern South Dakota with a grizzled old rancher, and asked him if his new pickup had put his saddle horse out of work.

"Like hell!" he growled. "I got a couple of pastures with deep grass where I don't dare use this damn new truck with its red-hot catalytic converter. Give me a horse ever' time, with its catalytic converter inside where it don't set the range afire!"

Though an occasional horse-drawn wagon can still be seen on smaller farms in the Soviet Union, most Soviet farming is fully mechanized. The breadbasket of the Soviet Union lies in the immense belt of The Steppes, which stretches from Eastern Europe to northeast Asia. The dark soils of these steppes are some of the richest in the

Beef cattle cluster on a ranch, or estancia, *in the Argentine pampa. Immense estancias dominate this humid grassland, one of South America's most fertile areas. The Spaniards brought livestock here in the 16th century; strays soon multiplied into vast wild herds that roamed the open range. Gauchos—South American cowboys—made their living off the herds, hunting them for cowhides and tallow, and occasionally for meat. But by the late 19th century, ranchers had divided the open range into private holdings.*

Today's gauchos still practice the art of steer roping (left), but now they work as hired hands on estancias.

world. Here farmers living and working on state or collective farms cultivate the black earth to produce mostly wheat, barley, sunflowers, and corn.

The collectivization of Soviet farms began in the late 1920s when Stalin forced peasants to give up their land to large socialized farms. These farms eventually assumed two forms: the sovkhoz, or state farm, where the worker receives a guaranteed salary from the government, and the

smaller collective, or kolkhoz, where members earn a share of the communal profits.

Some state farm complexes and larger kolkhozes look like factories, with dozens of silos, fleets of combines felling row after row of wheat, and high-rise concrete-block buildings that house workers. Others are less centralized, with farming families living in their own small wooden cabins or cottages within villages surrounded by communal fields.

Unlike most American farmers, who personally oversee the whole cycle of farming, Soviet farm workers perform specialized jobs, like factory workers. Ask a member of a cultivating brigade the protein content of cattle feed, and he or she probably won't be

Shades of autumn tint the foliage of a Crimean vineyard in Ukraine (left). Crimea produces many of the best Soviet wines, including sherry, Madeira, and port. Like most Soviet crops, grapes are grown and harvested on large collective and state farms worked by whole communities.

Modern machinery has not yet completely supplanted manual labor on some Soviet farms: In Ukraine, workers on the Hammer and Sickle farm still scythe and bundle wheat into sheaves by hand (above).

183

able to answer. That's the responsibility of the feeding brigade.

In their spare time, farming families are allowed to grow their own crops on small private plots and keep their own livestock: one cow, a calf, a pig, up to ten sheep, plus bees, rabbits, and chickens. After a day's labor, they turn to their gardens, cultivating every inch with potatoes, tomatoes, strawberries, raspberries, peaches, apples—crops they can keep or sell for profit at village markets. These gardens generate spectacular yields, producing almost 25 percent of the Soviet Union's output of vegetables, fruit, and livestock.

In recent years, Soviet leader Mikhail Gorbachev has initiated programs to decentralize the management of large Soviet farms by dividing them into smaller units, thus providing workers with more interest in the farms' success.

Change came late to the steppes of the Soviet Union compared with grasslands in other parts of the world. The original cover of these steppes was nutritious wild shortgrass that seemed to stretch forever, supporting roe deer, wild horses, and the saiga, a sheeplike antelope. Large areas of this cover survived well into the 20th century—but as need grew with the population, the wild steppes were broken.

Broken, too, are North America's grasslands. On the tallgrass prairies, some of the most productive grainlands in the world, very little natural tallgrass remains. To the west, some mixed-grass prairie lands survive, but farmers have largely replaced the wild midgrasses with tame analogues, such as wheat or grain sorghum, for this is the heart of the American wheat belt. The Great Plains were once a realm of shortgrasses that supported huge herds of bison; today, relatives of the bison—cattle—are still prime users of the plains. A large proportion of the plains survives as unbroken pasture, but as cattle overgraze, sagebrush and other tough shrubs have claimed broad reaches of shortgrass.

In the spring of 1934, the southern Great Plains were the scene of ecological disaster.

184

Blossoms and fresh produce lure shoppers to Bessarabskaya market in the Ukrainian city of Kiev. Built amid the rich soils of the steppes, Kiev is a center of agriculture and industry and the Soviet Union's third most populous city. Enterprising citizens tend small private plots in and around the city, then sell their harvest at the market for extra income.

NEXT PAGE: Flat land and rich soil make for good farming in the Red River Valley of eastern North Dakota. Glacial Lake Agassiz, which once covered this region, left behind a bed of black silty soil that now sprouts wheat, barley, and sunflowers.

185

For decades, farmers had managed their wheat crops carelessly, failing to rotate them or plow under the rich residues. Then, in the early 1930s, severe drought struck, and the wheat crops failed, leaving valuable fertile topsoil exposed. High winds lifted the topsoil and carried it as far east as the Atlantic Ocean. Millions of acres of farmland were transformed into near desert—the Dust Bowl—and thousands of farmers lost their livelihood.

Arctic winds sculpture snow-drifts on North Dakota's prairies (right). Blizzards that hit the plains from time to time may cause some damage, but the snow they bring is often welcomed as ground insulation during bitter winters.

In California's San Joaquin Valley, nature was only partly to blame for the 1977 dust bowl (above). Overgrazing, plowing, and removal of windbreaks left little defense against 100-mile-an-hour winds that damaged crops and stripped away millions of tons of soil.

Humans have a knack for degrading landscapes and seem bound to desertify biomes we ought to maintain with care. The Dust Bowl is an extreme example, but in almost every part of the world, dust is blowing in grasslands and savannas.

In the original semiarid savanna ecosystems of northern Africa and the Middle East, herds of cattle, sheep, and goats have overgrazed huge areas, converting them to desert or to savanna dominated by thorn scrub thickets—of little use to hoofed animals, domestic or wild.

Time is running out for many East African savannas. The Masai lived in relative harmony with the land for thousands of years, managing to maintain an ecological

Flying just seven feet off the ground, pilot Gary Gardner sprays weed killer on a field of spring wheat in north-central Kansas. Barnstorming daredevils pioneered crop-dusting in the 1920s, dumping insecticides out of barrels tied to their planes. Modern "aerial applicators" use sophisticated equipment to blanket fields with controlled amounts of fertilizer and pesticide. Since 1945 the use of agricultural chemicals worldwide has skyrocketed, producing larger harvests but also posing new problems for farmers. One major concern: Many weeds and insects have developed resistance to the chemicals, making the pests ever more difficult to control.

balance. From dry season to wet, they moved their herds between highlands and lowlands, allowing recently grazed land to recuperate and using the more fragile lowlands only during the rains. But beginning in the early 20th century, the Masai lost a large portion of their lush dry-season grazing lands to farmers and to national parks established to preserve wildlife. Now confined to a smaller area, many Masai are forced to graze their cattle all year long on dry lowlands that cannot withstand excessive use. The deterioration of this landscape affects all animals, both domestic and wild. The days of the great unspoiled savannas, teeming with herds of zebra, buffalo, and elephant, are numbered, as are those of the Masai. "So the land goes, and we go," says one Masai. "The land dies, and we die."

One alternative to herding in eastern Africa—large-scale farming—has met with even more trouble. Tropical and subtropical savanna soils aren't all that fertile to begin with, and once broken, they deteriorate rapidly under sun and rain. Efforts to convert large areas of this region to farmland have failed. In one such project, millions of acres of Kenya, Tanzania, and Zambia were plowed and planted with peanuts and sunflowers at an astronomical cost. The harvest was pitifully small.

n North America's Great Plains, the hard lessons taught by the Dust Bowl of the 1930s have not been forgotten. Still, in a fever of grain production, some farmers continue to break huge tracts of grassland for more wheat and larger surpluses: In 1987 I saw a new breaking of 10,000 acres of western South Dakota prairie. Out on the High Plains of western Kansas, Oklahoma, and Colorado, aquifers are being pumped dry by irrigation systems in order to raise surpluses of corn and wheat. In this mid-continental climate—where drought cycles, like tornadoes and blizzards, are facts of life—the potential for recurrent dust bowls is always present.

Much of the world's food is produced on grasslands that have been converted to grainfields or pasturage. We cannot live

191

Not much gets in the way of a determined farmer, not even the irregular slopes of southeastern Washington State (left). Farmers here use a hillside combine to harvest their wheat: The machine's hydraulic levelers keep the combine body level, while the header follows the sloping terrain, cutting and collecting the grain.

In northwestern Iowa, field hands work past sunset to put the July alfalfa crop to bed (above). In this region, this fast-growing crop usually produces two or three harvests a year.

193

without these lands, yet we sometimes treat them as if we could.

I often worry for grasslanders. The same open horizons and grassy solitudes that instilled much of their pride and independence, their solid, earthy self-confidence, have—paradoxically—also imparted a feeling of dependency and an awareness that for all their self-reliance, faith, and energy, they have never really been in charge of their land and livelihood. Bankers, politi-

cians, industrialists, all the powers that govern the marketplaces of individual nations and the world, also govern the grasslands and their people. In recent years those forces seem to have turned against grasslanders, and I worry about the weakening and loss of that fine level-eyed confidence in family and soil, that irreplaceable sense of self-worth.

Yet, for all the erosion of confidence and optimism, a kind of comfort arises from grasslands themselves, from the quiet dignity of fields and pastures. And the best way to dispel worry is to watch people at work in those fields, out there keeping faith with their land, under the long winds with the smell of distance in them.

194

JOHN MADSON

Industrial smoke stains the sky over downtown Winnipeg, a transportation hub on the eastern edge of Canada's Prairie Provinces. The great Canadian wheat belt, which sweeps some 800 miles west from Winnipeg, provides flat terrain for the Trans-Canada Highway linking Winnipeg with western Canada, and for a natural gas pipeline (above). Still incomplete, the pipeline will eventually transport natural gas from Alaska's North Slope across Canada to the contiguous United States.

It was evening of a day in other times, when the world was young. The People came to the river at last and lay down their burdens. Their trek from winter camp on the lee side of the mountain had been a long one, stalked by hunger and apprehension. The Old People and the Young Ones had begun to falter. But for most of the last day, eyes, ears, and noses had read the promising signs. The fishing birds flew overhead, with their piercing *kyew kyew kyew kyew kyew,* and the breeze bore the perfume of flowers and the tang of the hemlocks that stood near the water.

The 40 men, women, and children in the small clan hearkened to the roar of the falls, and the welcome sound lightened their footsteps. All day, as the trail descended to the river, they chattered excitedly. The Oldest Man had talked of starving times, when the river ran low. But now their ears told them that the water was high. They thirsted for its rushing-cold, tooth-tingling shock. Their bodies longed for the cleansing caress and the splashing good times ahead. And they wondered: When would the fish come, silver-bright, wild, and brave in their run from the sea?

On the rock face that overhung the river, opposite the place where the People always camped, someone—they knew only that it was one of the Ancestors—had carved a fish. From head to tail it was as long as four men, and marked out in red and white. Its open jaws hooked like talons and its body arched like a drawn bow. That night, before sleeping, the clan gathered to listen while the Oldest Man spoke to the great fish. He reminded the fish, reverently, as he did every year, of how the First Ancestor had liberated the fishes from the trackless ocean, and how the rivers and lakes carried them to multiply their kind in the high streams where they had been born.

After a few days the water at the foot of the falls shimmered and boiled with the salmon on their upstream journey. The fish leapt straight up, as though measuring the cascade—the height of a spear, and more—then leapt again, some to be thrown back by the torrent, springing again and again, others easily gaining the pool above, where they nosed into the swift current and swam out of sight.

The men readied their spears, with the deer-antler points tied to strong saplings. The women, with their knives, waited a respectful distance from the river, to receive the game and clean it. The first fat fishes would be roasted and everyone would feast. Later they would begin drying and smoking for winter stores and oiling the skins for watertight bags and clothing.

The Oldest Man chose a strong young boy to go first. As the boy raised his spear, his copper finger rings glittered in the sunlight. He struck. As soon as he had seized his prize from the water, and presented it to his mother as custom bound, all the men and boys joined in the hunt.

At dusk the People gathered around the fires where their savory meal awaited. The first salmon had been cut into many pieces, and as many men each ate one. The boy who had speared the first salmon put its tail back into the river, so that the fish would return next year. Then all the People had their fill. The Oldest Man spoke again, in gratitude to the fish for their willingness to be caught, in veneration to the river for making the salmon immortal.

This is how it was, in many places, in other times. Rivers of Ice Age Europe ran so thick with salmon that 10,000 could be caught in a day, and artists of the clans that followed the salmon painted totem fish on cave walls, along with bison, reindeer, and horses. When the scholar Giraldus Cambrensis traveled 12th-century Ireland, he found salmon leaps so abundant that he decided God had provided them for saints and pilgrims. All along the Pacific coast of North America, for hundreds of years, Indians greeted the running of the salmon with ritual and legend, and revered the fish as a sentient, superhuman being. In the 19th century, settlers along the Columbia drove their wagons across a river hub deep with migrating salmon.

It was Washington Territory then. In 1855 Indian leaders ceded to the white men stretches of riverside land on the Columbia. In return, the territorial governor declared, "The Indian will be allowed to take fish . . . at the usual fishing places . . . for as long as

The River Gan yields a harvest in southeastern China. On this Yangtze tributary, women gather water caltrop, a plant they cultivate for the leaves, which they feed to livestock, and for the appetizing, starchy fruit that appears at family meals. Across the world, rivers and their gifts sustain body and spirit. Humanity is the beneficiary where rivers flow.

PREVIOUS PAGE: The exuberance of youths diving into the monsoon-swollen Ganges at the holy city of Varanasi parallels the joy in rural India when the monsoon brings rain and fertile silt washing the land. The inundated temples honor Hindu deities: One of the greatest is the river, Mother Ganga.

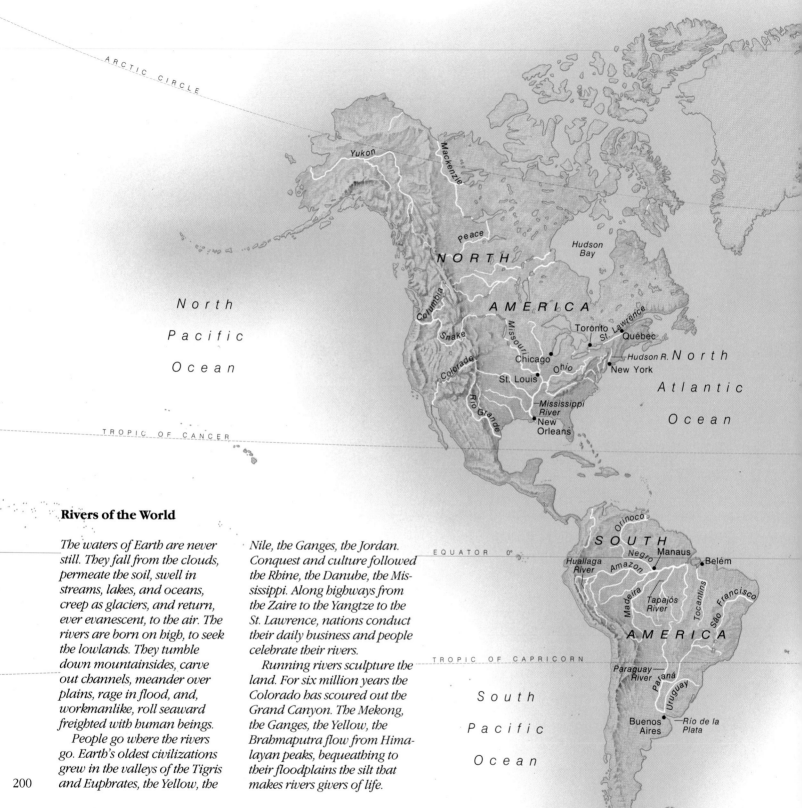

Rivers of the World

The waters of Earth are never still. They fall from the clouds, permeate the soil, swell in streams, lakes, and oceans, creep as glaciers, and return, ever evanescent, to the air. The rivers are born on high, to seek the lowlands. They tumble down mountainsides, carve out channels, meander over plains, rage in flood, and, workmanlike, roll seaward freighted with human beings.

People go where the rivers go. Earth's oldest civilizations grew in the valleys of the Tigris and Euphrates, the Yellow, the Nile, the Ganges, the Jordan. Conquest and culture followed the Rhine, the Danube, the Mississippi. Along highways from the Zaire to the Yangtze to the St. Lawrence, nations conduct their daily business and people celebrate their rivers.

Running rivers sculpture the land. For six million years the Colorado has scoured out the Grand Canyon. The Mekong, the Ganges, the Yellow, the Brahmaputra flow from Himalayan peaks, bequeathing to their floodplains the silt that makes rivers givers of life.

200

Ocean

North

Pacific

Ocean

Olenek

Indigirka

Kolyma

Yenisey

Lena

Amur

Northern
Dvina
River

Ob

Irtysh

Lake
Baykal

Shannon
R.

Thames
River

Dnieper
River

EUROPE

Don

Volga

A   S   I   A

London

Rhine

Paris

Vienna

Seine

Danube

Caspian Sea

Syr Dar'ya

Tarim

Amu Dar'ya

Black Sea

Yellow

Shanghai

Mediterranean Sea

Euphrates

Tigris

Srinagar

Hardwar

Yangtze

Gan.

Cairo

Brahmaputra

Jhelum

Li
River

Indus

Ganges

Dacca

Nile

Yamuna

Salween

Varanasi

Irrawaddy

Mekong

Sénégal

Timbuktu

Calcutta

Niger

AFRICA

Palar
River

Chao Phraya
River

Ho Chi
Minh City

Chari

White
Nile
River

Sudd

Blue Nile
River

Bangkok

Zaïre

Lake
Victoria

Sepik
R.

Indian Ocean

Zambezi

Okavango
River

Muckaninnie
Plains Swamp

Orange

AUSTRALIA

South

Atlantic

Darling

Murray

Ocean

The Huallaga River coils through the Peruvian rain forest on its way to join the Marañón—"the maze"—and, finally, the Amazon. The meanders change continually, cutting across themselves again and again to form oxbow lakes that trap fish and aquatic reptiles and mammals, making rich hunting grounds for the Indians of Amazonia. In the Amazon Basin, rain forest and floodplains support some 150,000 Indians. A Tukuna woman brings home dinner— a cayman—to her village near the Peruvian-Brazilian border. Indians hunt these reptiles in shallow water, killing them with spears, guns, bow and arrow, or their bare hands.

202

the sun shines, as long as the mountains stand and as long as the rivers run." There were 15 million salmon in the river every year then, and a few thousand people in the territory. Now there are only 2.5 million salmon, 2 or 3 times as many people, and the dammed rivers don't *run* any longer. And Indians serve jail sentences for fishing by the terms of the governor's promise.

A natural river is its own creator and its own creation. At each stage of its life, a river

origin bears an ancient mystique. It is the source of the power. It carries the lure of the unknown. The historian Herodotus admitted in the fifth century B.C. that he knew the sources of many rivers but not the Nile. The quest consumed famous lives and fortunes. Not until 1937 did it really end, when a little-known German explorer, Burkhart Waldecker, made his way to the Nile's southernmost source, a group of small springs on a mountainside in the tiny

has meaning for the people who live along it. A river may be born as an icy trickle of glacial melt, like the Rhône, or a boggy spring, like the Volga. It may spill from a lake as great as Baykal—as the Angara does—or as small as Itasca, the source of the Mississippi. The source may be a spring that bursts from a mountain slope, like the headwaters of the Shenandoah, or it may rise fitfully in a field, like the Thames.

A river's origin is its highest point. The

African country now known as Burundi.

A murmuring newborn stream traces across rocky outcrops and through mossy glades, gathering others like itself, rolling onward beneath the rains and the snows, until it makes a wide river. In its upper course it may scour gorges and canyons, digging deep into its own bed and creating the breathtaking scenery of the upper Yangtze or the Colorado. Constricted, the flow speeds up. It is the turbulent, oxygenated

203

As dusk falls on China's Li River, fishermen and trained cormorants follow their trade in a collaboration thousands of years old. The birds are strong swimmers, chase fish underwater, and snag the prey with hooked beaks. They perch in rank order on the edge of the bamboo raft. When the fisherman slaps the water with his oar, or signals with a distinctive cry, the excited cormorants dive into the river. A cord around the bird's neck ensures that it will swallow only the smallest fish and deliver others to its master for a reward. Lanterns may be used to lure fish to a circle of light, just as the eroded limestone peaks overlooking the Li have, for centuries, lured poets and artists.

white water of the river runner.

When the river descends from mountains it carries energy that people use to turn mill wheels and build cities. A river falling steeply into a plain may braid a multitude of minor channels with the main stream, like the Ganges as it falls from the Himalayas. Or it may braid as it crosses a plain—the Volga twists and untwists channels around low islands honed by the flowing water. Today the Volga islands at Volgograd offer a place for summertime fun; during World War II, they were a stronghold for Russians defending their city from the Nazi siege.

Almost surely, as a river slows and grades downward, it meanders. It leaves cutoffs and oxbows as offspring. "If you will throw a long, pliant apple-paring over your shoulder," wrote Mark Twain, "it will pretty fairly shape itself into an average section of the Mississippi River." Twain observed the Mississippi's habit of periodically taking a straight line across a meander, from one curl of the apple peel to another, so to speak. "More than once it has shortened itself thirty miles at a single jump!" he declared, adding that a man whose land was in the state of Mississippi might overnight find himself a taxpayer in Louisiana.

As regular as the seasons, a river may seethe in flood, moving mountains of silt that build its bed ever higher and leave a fertile, mileswide riverside plain.

A flowing river seeks the sea but may not find it. In an arid region, a river may meet its end through evaporation. It may seep away into sand or gravel like the undependable streams of western Australia, where sometimes nothing is left but the pools we sing of as billabongs in "Waltzing Matilda." It may pile up sediment in a marsh, as the Niger does, to create an inland delta that has nourished West Africa for centuries. But the Niger does not die in its first delta. Again replenished by tributaries, it runs on to the second, splitting into arms and channels that cover 14,000 square miles before they pile sediment at the mouth and pour river into the sea.

That is not the largest on Earth. The delta of the Ganges and Brahmaputra is twice as great, spreading over an area nearly the

The labor and skill of the fisherman have won food from the water since ancient times. The sturgeon, wrestled from its net in the Volga Delta, yields fine caviar the world has craved for centuries, and rich meat prized since the Stone Age. In Africa, on a Zaire-fed lake, a young Zairian fisherman presents a tilapia, a fish caught and cultivated along African rivers since Egypt of 2500 B.C. Tilapia swam among the fish that filled nets cast into the sea by the disciples when Jesus said to them, Come and dine.

207

size of England and Wales, and supporting some of the world's densest populations. This is a tidal mouth, an estuary, mixing fresh water with salt that surges, during the monsoon, in a ferocious, destructive wave nearly 30 feet high. The Amazon estuary-delta, covering 39,000 square miles, is the world's largest. The Brazilian Indians have a name for the thundering tidal wall of water that rolls inland 13 feet high, turning the river back upon itself, and tearing off trees and chunks of riverbank. They call it the big roar, the *pororoca.*

long the Amazon, all life beats to the rhythms of the greatest river on Earth. "I come from that generous land," wrote Brazilian Thiago de Mello, "where the men born of its lushness . . . are the brothers of . . . water, wind and hope." With an Indian guiding their canoe, de Mello was caught in one of the sudden, ferocious storms that blow over the river. Wind and rain whipped the men and the boat. Enormous tree trunks rode the waves, banging against the prow. "It was so dark that I could not see my hand a few centimetres away from my face, yet time and again I was certain that the Indian . . . managed to see something of the river and its banks in the midst of the pitch blackness. He was able to see or at least his ears or all his other very keen senses told him that something was coming towards the boat. For instance, he would suddenly bear to the left and then straighten up the craft again . . . while out of his half-open mouth there came a raucous cry, brief but powerful which, as if by a miracle, could be heard above the shrieking and howling of the storm."

For the Indians and the *caboclos*—rural people of the Amazon floodplain—the rains and the yearly floods dictate the terms of life. Caboclos are farmers, fishermen, miners, woodcutters. Itacoatiara, a town on a bluff downriver from Manaus, has grown in part because caboclo families have moved to town to escape problems that follow the river. In November or December, the rainy season begins. The water rises until it peaks at almost 30 feet in May or June.

By then the river has spread for miles across the *várzea*—the floodplain. Caboclos on the várzea live in houses raised on stilts. They must time the planting of their jute, maize, rice, sweet potato, and manioc at low water, and hope for a harvest before the fields are inundated. For the three to seven months of high water they herd their cattle long distances to dry land or crowd them into sheds on stilts or onto rafts, where the stress means that cows give less milk. The people must go out in boats to gather floating grasses for fodder.

It is an isolated existence, and the children get little or no schooling. When the men go out to fish, they leave wives and young children alone, sometimes for days. When the families move to Itacoatiara, the children can go to school—their parents want them to grow up to be more than poor peasants. The men may give up farming, they may work at odd jobs in a sawmill or a jute mill or a rubber plant, but, according to geographer Nigel Smith, who lived among them, they do not give up fishing.

A town fisherman gets up early. By four o'clock he is breakfasting on strong, sweet coffee and leftover fried fish. By five he has stopped at the tavern to meet the other men in his fishing group, and bought bread, cigarettes, and fishhooks, on credit if necessary. Then they are on their way in a small motor launch to the fishing grounds, perhaps in a nearby lake, along the riverbank, or in the flooded forest.

When the fishermen set out from the motorboat in canoes, they go in pairs or alone. True brothers of the water, they borrow hunting methods from the creatures they hunt. To bait the trotlines that they hang between submerged tree trunks, the men snatch tiny frogs from the mats of floating grasses. They lure swimming frogs onto the mats by flicking their fingers at the water's surface, imitating the sound of feeding carauaçú, predator fish that the frog flees—to be impaled on a hook as carauaçú bait.

Trotlines are specialized by bait and location. There are fish such as the tambaquí that depend on flood time, when they swim into the forest to eat seeds or fruit that fall from the trees. Both fishermen and fish relish the fruits of the socoró tree, and when a

Sampans carry Bangladesh villagers marooned by the flooding of the Brahmaputra, north of Dacca. The mixed blessing of the monsoon strands homes during the summer while its floods create seasonal paddies that increase the rice-growing capacity of this crowded, hungry land.

Native to the wetlands at the deltas of great Asian rivers, rice is one of humanity's most ancient cultivated plants, celebrated in myth and custom as a symbol of fertility and plenty. For billions of people, rice has been almost their only food. Today it sustains life for more than half the people on Earth.

With irrigation from the Mekong River, family farms in northeastern Thailand grow tobacco. Harvesting mature leaves (right), women usually dress traditionally and shield their faces against the hot sun and the strong, unpleasant smell, while men, in Western clothes, defy both.

The young woman drying mats of shredded tobacco leaves works with a profitable and popular crop. Some tobacco stays in the villages, where people make cigarettes for themselves. More is sold to processors. A government monopoly grows and processes most Thai tobacco from special "tobacco stations." Nearly half of northern and northeastern Thailand is planted in tobacco.

caboclo has found a good socoró, which he will use for bait as well as snacking, he tells no one where it is.

Danger awaits the caboclo who has laid a trotline for the largest fish of the Amazon. This is the piraíba, which can weigh as much as 300 pounds and can easily pull under the man trying to club it and haul it into a canoe. A man hunting pirarucú, a giant of almost 200 pounds, works alone. Perched in the prow of his canoe, he stalks across the water, paddling silently with one hand, harpoon poised in the other.

The fishermen may stay out for days, now and then meeting the motorboat to store their catch on ice. After dark, they fish with nets or gigs. At low water they cook a fish dinner and sleep on the riverbank, but during flood time there is nowhere to go. Man and canoe are one on the water. The fisherman arranges a base of water plants for his cooking fire, gleans firewood as he rows through the branches of várzea trees, roasts his catch on board, seasons it with pepper sauce, and eats it from a paddle. During storms he shelters himself under a tunnel of thatch or a plastic sheet.

The demons come out at night, none so awesome as *cobra grande,* a supernatural monster water snake. Caboclos say that cobra grande is hundreds of feet long and has luminescent blue eyes that mesmerize human beings, stealing their souls. It enchants canoes so that even the most strenuous paddling will not move them, and motorboats so that engines fail to make headway.

Nigel Smith found many spirits inhabiting the world of the várzea fisherman, among them *mãe de peixe,* the mother of fish. A fisherman can blame a poor catch on mãe de peixe, who protects her progeny. She may take the form of cobra grande, and wrest an overloaded net from the grasp of strong men. There was a man near Itacoatiara who had been out spearing fish night after night, possibly taking more than his share. As the fisherman pulled yet another fish from his spear, he saw a woman sitting in the stern of the canoe. He told Smith: "She was dark-skinned, with long black hair, and wore a deep red dress. She said nothing, looked in [my] eyes, and then vanished." The fisherman felt sick and quickly paddled home. He consulted a *pajé,* a spiritualist-healer, who said that the mother of fish had bewitched him.

Half a world away in West Africa, the people of the Niger—like the caboclos—fish,

Hunger rules the land where there is no rice. In a town in the Indian state of Tamil Nadu, men winnow rice from a harvest dependent on the beneficent rivers. Rice noodles nourish Hmong children whose only home is a refugee camp near Pak Chom, a Thai village on the Mekong. Across the river is Laos, where thousands of Hmong fled their mountain homes and a Communist government to live on lowlands along the Mekong. There, as in Tamil Nadu, on the rich alluvial soil of the floodplains people follow their yearly cycle, flooding seedbeds and paddies to grow rice, then draining them to harvest.

213

farm, and herd to the pulse of their river. When Niger farmers sow rice, they choose varieties that grow higher as floodwater rises, and ripen for harvest as the flood recedes. Farmers in different villages each have varieties best suited to their own topography and to the depth of floodwater they have learned to expect.

But never to trust. Floodplain farmers on the Niger and its tributaries play it safe by planting a field with several crops that need different amounts of water. If the flood is light, the beans and some sorghum will do well, but the rice will not grow. If the flood is deep, there may be no beans but rice and some sorghum will feed the families during the next year, and when the water goes down there will be pools left to irrigate onions, tomatoes, okra, and peppers.

All over West Africa there are old men and women who serve out their days as human scarecrows. They stand in grainfields, where youngsters have led them, and wave off birds they cannot see, their blindness an ugly gift of the rivers.

Simulium damnosum is a blackfly. Its bloodsucking bite transmits onchocerciasis, or river blindness, a disease that victimizes some 18 million people. Disease-carrying larvae enter and spread through the skin of a person who is bitten by the female fly. The larvae cluster in nodules where they mature and produce millions of microfilariae that migrate in the victim's skin, then die, causing sores and a debilitating—damnable—itching, so relentless that a badly infected person cannot sleep.

If the microfilariae reach the head, they create eye lesions that at best only impair eyesight, at worst cause blindness. The disease received its common name because the fly lays its eggs in fast-flowing streams where the larvae grow to become adult flies. Then they ride into the world on the bubbles of oxygen in white water.

In West Africa alone, the World Health Organization estimates, almost 100,000 people are permanently blind from the parasitic disease, and more than 2 million suffer infestation. It is too late for the blind but for others help has arrived. Since the mid-1970s the World Health Organization has conducted the "oncho program," a success-

The Ganges flows in the streets during the summer monsoon, complicating life for the citizens of Varanasi and a rickshaw driver who slogs through the turbid overflow. In 1978 the river rose 50 feet above its normal level in Varanasi, and for many weeks was 10 miles wide here. Monsoons directly affect the economic prosperity of India and half the world. Although heavy downpours can destroy a harvest, floodplain crops depend on these seasonal rains that bring the promise of renewed life in the form of fresh deposits of rich silt.

Dungas *along the Jhelum: Covered barges hug the bank in Srinagar, India. Dunga crews and their families live in the boats and carry tourists and timber on the Jhelum in the mile-high Kashmir Valley.*

Bangkok's canals (opposite), for centuries the city's main arteries, are still the route preferred by many Thai. A boatman paddles a traditional flat-bottomed boat past a house built on stilts to protect it from seasonally rising water. A girl plays in her liquid front yard under a spirit house—a miniature temple that hangs in most Thai houses and shelters guardian spirits. South of Bangkok the Chao Phraya River, which feeds the canals, flows into a fertile delta.

216

ful aerial spraying of fast rivers in more than ten countries of West Africa. Infection has dropped dramatically. Then, in 1987, came ivermectin, a medication in the form of a simple pill that prevents the worms from reproducing and kills the microfilariae. Its manufacturer, Merck & Co., Inc., plans to distribute ivermectin—at no cost—in whatever amounts are necessary to end the torment and eliminate river blindness completely.

The river speaks: *The Floodtime's mine, the Slacktime's mine, by me is runoff made . . . The silt's my form at time of Flood. . . . I am the whole, the whole I am. . . . for I am Nile.* For 7,000 years the valley of the god-river has made an isolated world for Earth's most enduring civilization. A strip of green land clings to the edges of green and blue water, winding—in Egypt—for 750 miles between cliff and rock and desert to the apex of the 8,500-square-mile delta. Along the sinuous strip and in the delta, villages are home to the fellahin, or farmers.

"I am a fellah," said Anwar Sadat of his childhood in a delta village. Sadat wrote of the fellahin self-sufficiency and peace of mind that came from an irradicable "sense of home." In the delta villages, Egyptian culture has long mixed with other cultures, from the Greek and Roman to the French and the British. Fellahin there have had more than a century to adapt to the perennial irrigation that dams brought to the old way of agriculture.

In Upper Egypt the fellahin live at a slower pace, "isolated in space and time," in the words of journalist Richard Critchfield. On all sides lie the empty desert and great stone temples of the pharaohs, "unaltered for thousands of years."

Only in the mid-1960s did a power greater than the Nile enter their lives. It was then that the High Dam at Aswan began storing water. For the first time in thousands of years the river did not have its way. The an-

217

218

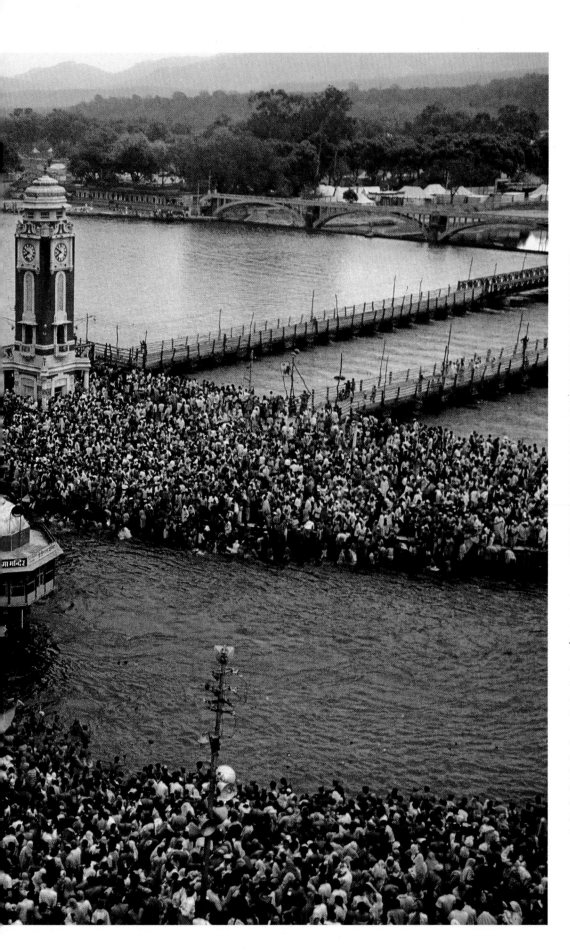

Zealous Hindus mass on the banks at Hardwar to celebrate their New Year by visiting temples and bathing in the Ganges. The river flows through the heart of Hindu myth and Indian life, providing water for religious rituals as well as for irrigation, power, and bathing.

Praying at Varanasi, a father and son seek to purify body and soul in the sacred river. Ganges water, taken home in brass vessels, is sprinkled on shrines and drunk—polluted though potable, say the faithful, because of its holiness.

nual flood would come no more. No longer would silt spread across the land that had always stood in the human mind as the emblem of Earth's fertile floodplains. Instead the fellahin use chemical fertilizer. With irrigation year-round, they grow two or three crops a year instead of one as before, although it is not always easy to get them to market. Egypt's burgeoning population needs more food and the increased electrical power generated by the High Dam. But the pull of the old rhythms is strong.

Shahhat, An Egyptian, Critchfield's study of life in an Upper Nile village, demonstrates this eloquently. Shahhat is a young fellah who works his land skillfully. Barefoot, in his loose white cotton pants, he uses a short-handled hoe, a wooden winnowing fork, a shadoof, and other tools of pharaonic times. His village is a place of dark passions, blood feuds and drunken fights, extravagance and debt, cruelty to women. It is also a place of hospitality and generosity, music and feasting, family strength and honor. And a visceral identification with the river: Shahhat's father, near death, asks for a drink of Nile water.

One hot day Shahhat swims in a canal. "The maize on the further bank glistened gold from the slanting sun; the dust shone golden in its wide rays; the mud of the bank was thickly overgrown with hyacinth weed; hundreds of greenish-brown snails bobbled up and down at the water's edge."

The snails carry worms that cause bilharzia, or schistosomiasis. The worms pierce the skin and lay eggs that travel in the bloodstream to the liver and other organs. Complications range from lethargy and pain to kidney failure and spinal cord damage. Bilharzia is thought to affect 4 percent of all the people in the world—in Egypt as many as 50 percent. It is not a new gift of the Nile—mummies and tomb carvings show bilharzia to be thousands of years old.

The villagers use the canals for drinking, bathing, irrigation, washing animals and clothes, and they reinfect the snail hosts by passing eggs when they urinate into the water. Shahhat's fatalism is common: "If I get bilharzia, I get bilharzia!"

As he grows to manhood, Shahhat must decide whether to look for work in Cairo or to stay in the village. He wanders into the hills to think. "He could see . . . the two crumbling stone giants of the Colossi of Memnon, . . . the canyon into the cliffside temple of Hatchepsut, and winding above it, the trail up the ridge and down again to the Valley of the Kings. . . . Around a bend in the river, he could see the white sails of three feluccas. To Shahhat, the Nile was *el Bahr,* the sea, the giver of life.

". . . Shahhat wondered what his life would have been like if the river had not been tamed. Poorer, but lived in the old natural rhythms and certainties. For the dam had brought the incessant field work, even in hottest summer. It had brought the diesel pumps, the fights to load sugar cane, the feuds and frustrations." But he would stay at home. "Everything is from Allah," he concluded. "I cannot decide anything. Everything we are is from him."

F lood is the archetypal human disaster. Genesis recounts: *And the rain was upon the earth forty days and forty nights. And the waters prevailed exceedingly upon the earth; and all the high hills, that were under the whole heaven, were covered. . . . And every living substance was destroyed.*

The Nile has often shown its might. When it burst through a levee during an 1887 flood, fellahin stood shoulder to shoulder, trying to stem the water with cornstalks and with doors and windows torn from houses. The Yellow River, fanning across northern China's Great Plain, figures in the records more terribly than any other river on Earth. Although there have been no major floods since 1960 (thanks to a new dam), at least 1,500 times in the last three and a half centuries the Yellow has brought tragedy to the people of the dusty, yellow loess plateau. Legends look back to a 13-year rampage in the 23rd century before Christ. In 1887 and 1888 a Yellow River torrent raged for two months and caused the death of at least a million people from drowning, disease, and starvation when crops failed. Cities, towns, and farms in a 50,000-square-mile area lay under 20 to 30 feet of water.

Amid smoke from funeral pyres, attendants prepare a corpse for cremation. To die in Varanasi is for a Hindu a sacred consummation. Thousands of pilgrims come here each year to spend their last days, to be cremated in soul-purifying flames, and to have their ashes scattered on the Ganges. In Hindu belief, the god Shiva, said to dwell in Varanasi, frees the soul from the cycle of reincarnation.

Families that cannot afford a big fire push their dead into the river half cremated. City officials have proposed electric crematoriums, but doms—*who perform the funeral rites and sell the expensive firewood—call the reform a breach of ancient Hindu custom.*

With a flourish of paddles, men of Papua New Guinea embark on a pig hunting expedition along the Sepik River. Their ritually decorated canoes can be 50 feet or more in length.

Contending with floods every year, tropical riverine peoples have long depended on canoes. An Australian Aboriginal family (top) debarks a eucalyptus tree to fashion a hunting canoe for the Muckaninnie Plains Swamp. Along Botswana's Okavango River (right) a master of the adz carves a dugout from a hardwood trunk. In two weeks, under skillful hands, a tree can become a fishing boat, a cargo carrier, or a taxi.

Emperors and generals have long used the Yellow as a weapon. In the summer of 1938 it was a two-edged weapon that led to Chiang Kai-shek's being compared to "a god playing with a water hose." To stop the Japanese Army, Chiang ordered his Nationalist troops to blast a break in the levee that would send a flood against the enemy. The deluge stopped the Japanese. It also spread across thousands of square miles, killed 900,000 Chinese, and sent refugees wandering across a devastation that lasted for years. The land was reclaimed under slogans of the People's Republic proclaiming, "Control the Yellow River" and "Turn the Curse into a Blessing."

Most of the rivers on Earth have been made to behave—"tamed" we say, in recognition of their natural power. But not all. The Arno flows through the 2,000-year-old city of Florence, Italy, a city that has seen hundreds of Arno floods. Florence lies in a basin, below hard clay hills that were deforested centuries ago. In early November 1966 heavy rain was falling on the Arno watershed. During a night and a day, water rose as high as 20 feet in the buildings, and roared through the streets in rubble-laden cataracts. When it receded, mud and debris covered the city and its priceless store of Renaissance art, books, and manuscripts. The city welcomed the students and scholars from around the world who came to help rescue and restore the treasures.

In the United States, millions of people live in floodplain towns or other settlements that are vulnerable to flooding. During the 1970s more Americans died in flash floods than in hurricanes, tornadoes, or any other catastrophe of nature. This is a grim record but it inspired more efficient prediction and warning systems.

In 1927, during the great Mississippi flood, couriers carried the alarm through an Arkansas town, racing from house to house, shouting that an upstream crevasse was about to send water pouring six feet deep through town. The streets were dry at noon. By two o'clock mules drowned, still hitched to their wagons.

This flood, judged by Secretary of Commerce Herbert Hoover, to be "the greatest peace-time (Continued on page 230)

224

A Nile ferry—five barges and a stern-wheeler—makes its way through the Sudd, an area in southern Sudan of shallow lakes and sinuous channels. "Some evil spirit," wrote explorer Samuel Baker of the Sudd, "appears to rule in this horrible region of everlasting swamp." These steamers can carry a thousand people on a 900-mile trip in six days, but clogging vegetation may stretch the trip to six weeks. Despite its difficulties, this section of the upper Nile is one of humanity's most ancient routes.

Like the Nile, the Chao Phraya is a vital highway for goods and people. Thai workers load rice onto a ship at the river's mouth in Bangkok.

NEXT PAGE: Freighters steam past the industrial skyline of Quebec City on the St. Lawrence River, gilded by an autumn sunset. The St. Lawrence Seaway, at 2,350 miles the world's longest inland waterway, links the Great Lakes with the Atlantic Ocean and makes seaports of inland cities such as Toronto, Detroit, and Chicago.

225

227

The Glen Canyon Dam in northern Arizona, since its completion in 1964, has backed up the Colorado River to hold water for irrigation, drinking, electricity, recreation, and tourism. The bizarre result is that houseboats like this one on Utah's 186-mile-long Lake Powell now harbor on sandstone cliffs that once soared high above the river. A multitude of artificial lakes and reservoirs in the region has led to the jest that Arizona has more boats per capita than any other state.

disaster in our history" is not quite history to many people. They were there. Some Southerners believed that the Great Lakes had burst, and no wonder. They lived in the spout of a funnel carrying tons of water the river would not hold. By summer a dirty, swirling yellow sea 1,000 miles long, and as much as 80 miles wide and 18 feet deep, covered parts of 7 states.

To journalists there was the "thrill of airplane roaring overhead" as pilots scouted

marooned houses and farms for survivors. "Wires, radio,...speed boats, and motor cars" alerted thousands of families who fled homes and farms for levee-top tent-cities. Stern-wheel steamers cruised among inundated treetops, picking up victims. Sawmills turned out a thousand small rescue boats in ten days. Coast Guard cutters dashed about, picking up people spotted by Navy and Marine aircraft. Barges hauled people, furniture, and livestock. Animals either drowned or clambered up to levees and empty buildings. Trains crept along submerged tracks, carrying refugees in boxcars. Convicts under the gun piled sandbags to strengthen the banks. Cajuns, the people of the bayou, rode out the flood

230

Once considered derelict, London's Docklands have become fashionable. On the Isle of Dogs (right), erstwhile grounds for royal hunting hounds, new homes, marinas, shops, and pubs now rise from the ruins of old warehouses and shipyards. Though Thameside buildings bring top prices in Docklands, the river can spell disaster as well. Rising tides and flood danger led to the construction of the Thames Barrier (above). Piers house machinery that can raise a 60-foot-high steel wall to hold back the surging sea.

in shanty boats. People in the camps sang "Throw Out the Lifeline" and "Shall We Gather at the River?"

Since then the river world has been channelized, dammed, and, yes, tamed. Every year so many new dams are built—at least 500—that, according to one study, by the year 2000 more than 60 percent of the world's river water will be flowing only where, when, and if human beings allow it to. Reservoirs stand deep over places where people lived and died with rivers—over houses and towns and villages, over camps and trails and hunting grounds, over graves and sacred places where people worshiped the gods of the rivers.

The Mississippi has higher levees. For mile after mile its banks are artificial, overlaid by concrete mattresses that won't erode like a natural bank. The river, given its own way, would spill into the Atchafalaya channel, abandoning New Orleans and Baton Rouge as it has abandoned smaller towns in the past. But the U. S. Army Corps of Engineers is watching, "fighting Mother Nature," in their words, to save the American economy, or at least the portions of it represented by the oil and chemical companies along the river between those two cities, and by the shippers of grain and ore that use the waterway. Efficient transportation is vital, as is access to the port of New Orleans, where thousands of foreign oceangoing ships call each year.

Life has changed for the salmon, too. Some live on ranches. In a hatchery on a Columbia tributary, salmon ranchers raise fingerlings to smolt size. Then the ranchers load the fish into tank trucks and drive them to artificial ponds near the coast. Soon the salmon learn the chemistry of the pond water, just as the wild smolt learns the smell and taste of its natal stream. Then the ranch salmon are turned into the ocean to feed themselves. At maturity, after as long as three years at sea, and by the mysterious homing instinct that we understand only a little better than did our Ice Age ancestors, the survivors obediently come back to the right pond, where a 20th-century reception—and no reverence—await them.

Sheep graze on the Isle of Dogs, heedless of the commuter train and the fast track of change in London's eastside Docklands. The eight-square-mile Docklands shows many such contrasts as it moves from defunct Thameside docks to upscale commercial properties. With a decayed building for a backdrop, the busy life of a Brick Lane market goes on apace. Windsurfers glide past cargo cranes and the new homes of papers that have moved from the City—the Daily Telegraph *and* Sunday Telegraph.

233

Most of the homecomers go to the canning factory or the gourmet grocer. The best are selected for breeders. The brood females, of course, don't scoop nests with their tails in the gravel of a swift streambed, as the wild salmon do, they don't lay eggs for the males to fertilize, they don't perish like the wild salmon whose strength is spent. But they do die. A technician removes the eggs and the milt and does the fertilization by gently mixing them together. Someone else grinds up the meat for fish food back at the ranch.

Henry David Thoreau wrote in 1847 of the Merrimack shad, thwarted in their migrations by a dam and a canal and the factories of Lowell, Massachusetts. Thoreau suggested that "after a few thousands of years, if the fishes will be patient," nature will redress the wrong by leveling the dam and the factories and cleaning the river.

Maybe it won't take thousands of years. Nature is at last getting some help. No one can regret dams, now that people are protected from tragic flooding. Nor can we thrive without the electricity that dams give us. But we do recognize that, godlike, we have appropriated nature's creative power, and that there is a way to pay the debt, to give thanks. All over the world, as we begin to take care of rivers, we find that they rejuvenate us. We affirm their blessing. We know the spell that water has upon us, flowing clean and wild and free, a river making its own way through our lives.

234

MARGARET SEDEEN

London's modern shapes squeeze in on an old landscape. A new million-pound condominium (left) faces the 19th-century Tower Bridge. Common in the redeveloped Docklands, such flats can double in value in a year. Easy access to downtown London has made the Docklands an attractive location for young professionals. While critics charge that inflated prices will drive away local people, a new factory on the Isle of Dogs reflects the shape of things to come.

235

LIVING IN

HIGHLANDS

hy do people live in the highlands of the world, in homelands often isolated and harsh, overshadowed by grand and ominous peaks? Some simply stay where their parents stayed, and their parents' parents, as far back as anyone remembers. But sometimes families, tribes, and clans move upland because they choose to, or because they must.

From the mile-high peaks of Luzon that protected the Ifugao people from Spanish conquistadores to the rugged passes of Pakistan's North-West Frontier, where Afghan families today await peace, mountain niches have long offered refuge to people fleeing oppression. In 1838 bands of Cherokees hid in the dense, misty forests of the Great Smokies to escape the savage forced eviction westward we know as the Trail of Tears. They survived, and today their descendants own 56,000 acres of slopes and ridges which, their myth says, were carved from the Earth by the dipping wings of the great grandfather buzzard.

For 4,000 years Chinese expansion in Southeast Asia pushed beleaguered Hmong tribes away from their lives as lowland rice farmers, and into the highlands, where they prospered as "kings of the mountains." Though ravaged by 20th-century wars, some struggle to maintain their independent culture in the mountains they love. Many who come because they must, stay because they choose to.

Highlands cover about a quarter of Earth's land surface. In the United States we tend to reserve mountains for parks, wilderness, timberland, and national forests. From Denali National Park and Preserve in Alaska to the Great Smokies in Tennessee and North Carolina, mountainous regions are set aside for the recreation of the human body and spirit. But in most parts of the world, mountains and highlands are home and livelihood. About 10 percent of Earth's people live more than 3,000 feet above sea level.

What is the difference between highlands and mountains? A *mountain* rises conspicuously above the surrounding land and tapers to a peak. The Himalayas clearly are mountains, the highest on the land. Though they rise no more than 11,000 feet above the surface around them, their peaks average 20,000 feet above sea level. North America's Appalachians are also mountains, where the highest peak, Mount Mitchell in North Carolina, reaches only 6,684 feet.

Highlands generally are regions that rise more gradually in gentle uplands, rolling foothills, and—often abruptly—in high plateaus. But highlands may also include rugged cliffs, steep valleys, and mountains.

One striking characteristic of mountain environments is the decrease in temperature with altitude. We are all familiar with the image of mountain climbers clinging to a snow-blasted peak. Although most of us will experience nothing so dramatic, a drive into the mountains will demonstrate the same principle: On average, the temperature drops about 3.5 degrees for every thousand feet above sea level.

Wherever colonial rulers have gone in the tropics, they have sought refuge from the lowland heat in high retreats. Many hill stations, such as Baguio in the Philippines, a resort for Americans and wealthy Filipinos, or Nuwara Eliya in Sri Lanka—where 19th-century British tea planters golfed and gardened—are only 5,000 or 6,000 feet high, but that is enough to lower the temperature about 20 degrees. Mount Kenya in East Africa rises near the Equator; its foothills are fertile farmland, but year-round ice crowns its 17,000-foot twin peaks. Even well below this elevation in middle or high latitudes, especially in winter, snow accumulates and glaciers may form.

When people climb mountains, they notice that breathing becomes more difficult the higher they go. Atmospheric pressure is lower. In other words, the air becomes "thin." At 16,000 feet, a lungful of air may contain only half the oxygen as at sea level. People newly arrived in mountains often suffer from dizziness, headaches, and nausea because their bodies cannot efficiently use the little oxygen they do get. Mountain climbers may feel these effects acutely. After the first successful climb of Mount Everest, in 1953, expedition leader Sir John Hunt described the effects of oxygen depri-

A frosted Himalayan ridge rises behind the village of Bashist, India, where wheat farmers and dairy herders live in slate-roofed cedar houses above their ground-floor cattle pens. Here in the fertile Kulu Valley—once called the end of the habitable world—villagers earn extra money by hiring themselves out as porters for the mountain climbers who follow their valley up into the snow-blown Himalayas.

PREVIOUS PAGE: About 150 miles north of Bashist, in India's remote Ladakh district, a teamster drives his donkeys over a 15,000-foot Himalayan pass. Heavy snows seal routes into Ladakh for months at a time, isolating the villagers.

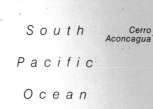

Earth's High Places

In their massive grandeur, mountains seem ageless and invincible, but many ranges have risen and fallen in the four billion years since the first volcanic cones pocked the globe. Most of today's high mountains formed within the past 100 million years, when continents collided, buckling and cracking, as the rigid plates of the Earth's crust shifted. Forces we don't fully understand continually shape the mountains: Volcanoes erupt or collapse, and earthquakes rattle peaks, ranges, and cordille-

ras like the Andes, which began to rise 180 million years ago, when the heavy floor of the Pacific Ocean wedged below the thick continental crust of South America. The Appalachians are remnants of collisions some 300 to 400 million years ago of North America against Europe and then Africa. They may have reached Alpine heights before erosion wore them down. In time, the Alps and Himalayas will also crumble, carved by water, ice, and wind—a process humans are ultimately powerless to halt.

Arctic

ARCTIC CIRCLE

North
Pacific
Ocean

North
Atlantic
Ocean

ALASKA RA.
Mt. McKinley

COAST MOUNTAINS

ROCKY MOUNTAINS

CASCADE RA.

SIERRA NEVADA

NORTH
AMERICA

Sacramento

Weirton

APPALACHIAN MOUNTAINS

Mt. Mitchell

Creel

SIERRA MADRE OCCIDENTAL

SIERRA MADRE ORIENTAL

TROPIC OF CANCER

GUATEMALAN
HIGHLANDS

GUIANA
HIGHLANDS

EQUATOR   0°

SOUTH
AMERICA

ANDES

BRAZILIAN
HIGHLANDS

La Paz

TROPIC OF CAPRICORN

South
Pacific
Ocean

Cerro
Aconcagua

ANDES

Ocean

EUROPE

Trolltindane

Moscow

ALPS
Obergurgl
Bedizzano
PYRENEES

Canary
Islands

Mediterranean Sea

ATLAS MOUNTAINS

CARPATHIAN
MOUNTAINS

BALKAN
MTS.

CAUCASUS
MTS.
El'brus

ZAGROS MOUNTAINS

URAL MOUNTAINS

A S I A

VERKHOYANSK RANGE

KOLYMA RANGE

ALTAY MTS.

PAMIRS

TIAN SHAN

LADAKH
Kulu
Pokhara
Mt. Everest
Darjeeling

HIMALAYAS

Liping

North

Pacific

Ocean

AFRICA

Manakhah

JABAL HARAZ

ETHIOPIAN
HIGHLANDS

KENYA
HIGHLANDS
Mt. Kenya
Kilimanjaro

WESTERN GHATS

Sri
Lanka
Nuwara
Eliya

Baguio

Luzon
Philippines

Ramu River

New
Guinea

Indian Ocean

South

Atlantic

Ocean

HAMERSLEY
RANGE

AUSTRALIA

GREAT DIVIDING RANGE

Mt. Kosciusko

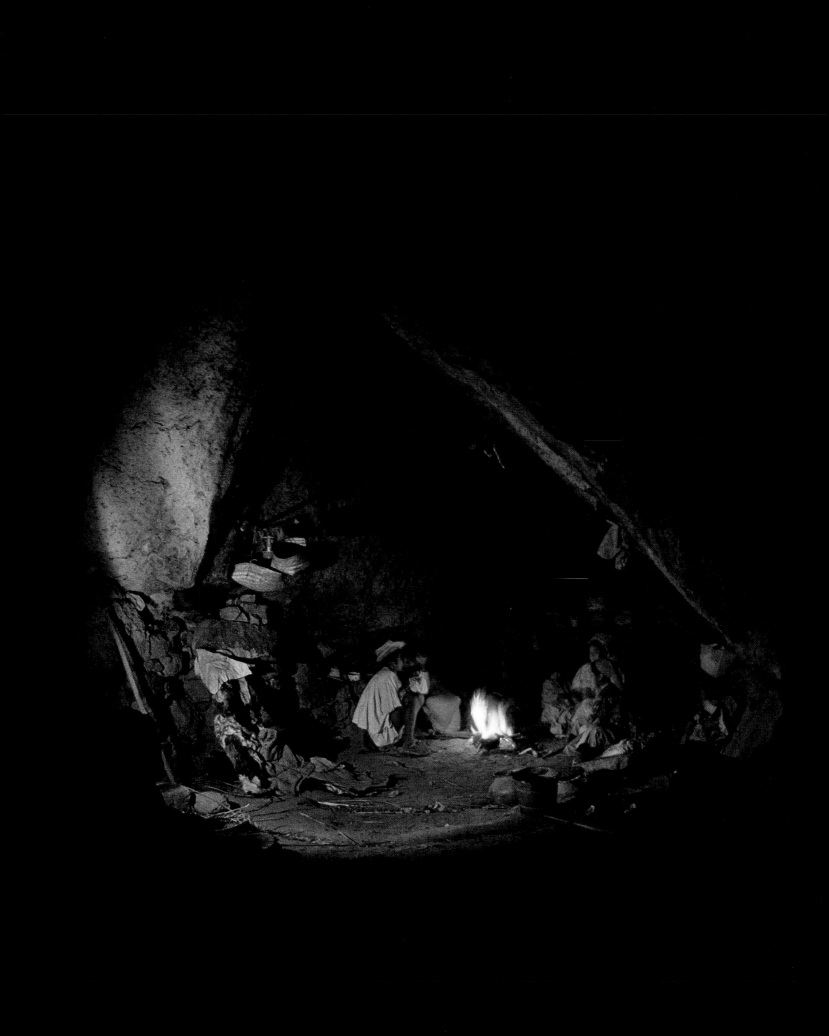

vation: "Above 25,000 feet, the climber's heavy legs seem riveted to the ground, his pulse races, his vision blurs, his ice ax sags in his hand like a crowbar. To scoop up snow in a pan for melting looms as a monumental undertaking."

People who have lived for generations at high altitudes become adapted to the thin atmosphere. The Andean Indians have barrel-like chests with large lungs and hearts, and a high breathing rate, all of which increase their ability to get and use oxygen. These physiological adaptations are much like those made by athletes in training who condition their muscles to perform under stress. For the Andeans, high altitude does not diminish the capacity for hard work—or play; a favorite sport in the Andes is the strenuous game of soccer.

Ruggedness of terrain is the essence of mountains. Hmong tribesmen in the highest mountains of northern Laos sometimes tether themselves to stumps in order to plant their steep fields without tumbling out of them. Farmers in the Alps used to secure themselves with rope to scythe hay. Appalachian farmers joke about harvesting their potatoes by rolling them downhill, and claim that when they cut firewood they can toss it directly into the chimney.

In Mexico's northern Sierra Madre, Tarahumara Indians keep the home fires burning, even when home is a cave. Many Tarahumara live in log cabins high in the mountains most of the year but in winter move down to warm rock shelters. Caves provide year-round homes for some Tarahumara like the family who walled in the space beneath an overhanging rock (right) outside the town of Creel. Wherever they dwell, these self-reliant farmers live simply, with no furniture and few possessions beyond pots, baskets, blankets, stones for grinding corn, and earthenware jars for making corn beer.

The mountain fastness that serves as a refuge also acts as a cultural barrier. Modern roads, automobiles, radio, telephones, and television have reduced isolation, but large and complex mountain systems such as the Andes, Caucasus, Himalayas, and Alps still contain diverse cultures, nationalities, and languages. In Switzerland, as late as 1940, there persisted more than 35 dialects of German, French, Italian, and even a Latin tongue known as Romansh.

In the anthology *Mountain People*, writer and child psychiatrist Robert Coles has described a summer he spent in an isolated Appalachian hollow, a visit that taught him the error of his "blind and ignorant" city opinions about the hill people of Kentucky, West Virginia, and North Carolina. Books had convinced him that he would be "slumming" among a people of hopeless

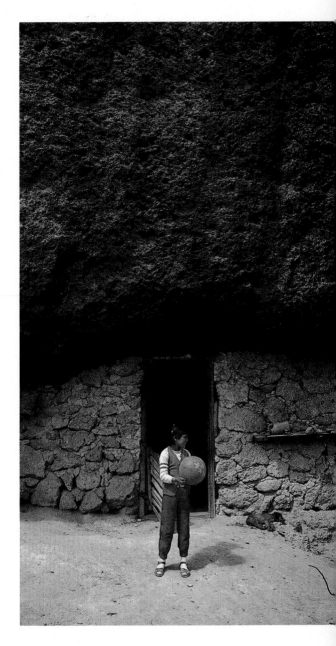

In Papua New Guinea's Southern Highlands, Mendi men and boys build a house with walls of woven pitpit. Workers pound the reed with wooden mallets, split and flatten it for weaving, and attach the plaited walls to a picket frame. The Mendi often build double walls, packing the space with leaves and reeds for insulation against the cool nights common above 5,000 feet.

Bundles of kunai grass tied to bamboo rafters form waterproof thatch roofs. To save heat, and kill thatch-eating beetles,

the Mendi forgo chimneys and simply allow smoke to seep out through the roof. Houses deteriorate in the rainy climate, and the men must build new ones every few years.

The Mendi live in clans whose houses and gardens are often scattered over areas as large as ten square miles. Men and boys from the age of seven or eight sleep in houses apart from their families, a custom that developed as a defense during centuries of frequent ritual war with neighbors over land, pigs, and women.

244

245

superstition and suspicion. But an articulate 13-year-old boy showed Coles an ethical and spiritual life that grew directly from the mountains that were his home.

"We're sent [into this life] to ask, and to find, the right way to live. Christ told us, and He went on a mountain when he told us, remember.... Sometimes, when the clouds are real low, they almost touch you, standing on the big mountain. Then there'll be the mist, and the drizzle, and my grandmother says they are messages from God; He's touching you, He's so close by. So you go back down the mountain and you remember. Yes, you remember where you are, and what you've got to do! There's all those chores, and they're for you to do, and God is watching!"

Ages before the first westering Yankees settled in the Appalachians, native North Americans were making a living by hunting and gathering. Both east and west, the mountains were natural extensions of lowland hunting grounds. Archaeological evidence suggests that, in summer, Plains Indians moved from the dry lowlands to the cooler, damper mountains in search of deer and bighorn sheep. Their migrations were usually seasonal, but in times of drought they probably moved to higher land seeking water and game.

Over the millennia people began to shift from hunting and gathering to the cultivation of crops and the domestication of animals. Mountains helped in the shift because they offer a greater variety of environments within short distances.

The first farming may have resulted when certain aboriginal geniuses, probably women, made the connection between wild grass seeds brought to campsites for food, and the wild grasses that sprouted where some of those seeds had been spilled. Early mountain dwellers found ways to domesticate the food plants most valuable to humanity. They grew corn in highland Mexico, rice in the mountains of eastern Asia, wheat and barley in the Zagros Mountains of Iran, and in the Andes, potatoes, squash, and beans.

247

In a Mendi women's house, men sit on planks outlining their domain. The old, bearded clan leader's two wives and his son's three wives live here with their young children, sleeping on wooden platforms with log neck rests and pandanus-leaf mats. The pen at rear holds some of the 22 squealing pigs that also share the house. Women rear the pigs tenderly, hand-feeding and even suckling orphaned piglets.

Most Papuan highlanders practice polygamy. Mendi men marry as many wives as they can afford. Bride prices can exceed a thousand dollars or 80 pigs. Though they sleep apart, Mendi parents rendezvous regularly in the privacy of the bush to produce large families.

In Italy's Apuan Alps, scarred marble peaks rise behind the stone houses of Bedizzano. For 2,000 years rock near the town has yielded Carrara marble, prized by architects and artists for its fine grain. Like their fathers and grandfathers, most men here are quarriers. Their callused hands and missing fingers attest to the rigors of slicing marble from mountains with wires coated with abrasive slurry. Until recently, multi-ton slabs rode downhill on wooden sleds, and runaway loads crushed many quarriers. Today trucks do the hauling. To negotiate hairpin turns, drivers must alternate between forward and reverse gears to zig and zag up and down the switchbacked quarry roads.

248

Sheep, goats, yaks, and llamas are all adapted to rocky terrain, sparse vegetation, and thin, cold air. People found yet another way to exploit rocky uplands when they domesticated these animals. The livestock could harvest scattered vegetation and turn it into milk, meat, fats, hides for clothing, and many other things that made life more comfortable. So productive was this system that some people became entirely pastoral, following their herds and taking from them most of the necessities of life.

Highland farming reaches its finest development in the humid tropics. Usually the climate is stable year-round and people can concentrate their efforts on the continual use of their land. Often this means that they build terraces. These may be simple furrows cut along a contour or they may be stone-walled ridges as high as 20 feet, carefully engineered into the slope, where they may climb for a thousand feet or more.

Terraces break a hillside into stairsteps that retard erosion and increase the area of arable land. Often terrace farmers build irrigation systems so that water from mountain streams can benefit plots the entire way down as it trickles from one level to another. Also, terraces can be warmer, since they may intercept the sun's rays at a higher angle than the original slope would. Irrigation water also holds heat and gives overnight protection from freezing, so people can usually farm irrigated terraces at higher elevations than they can farm dry fields.

Building some terraces takes such engineering skill, organization, and cooperation that it is an enterprise comparable to the construction of the Egyptian Pyramids. The terracing of entire mountainsides has taken decades, even centuries.

In Switzerland, in Peru, on Tenerife in the Canary Islands, people drove pack animals and toiled up the mountainsides themselves, carrying alluvial soil and manure on their backs. The geographer Ellen Churchill Semple called this "desperate agriculture." In some places even today it is an endless task. Every year, Peruvian farmers retrieve the soil that has washed down the slopes from their terraces, each farmer, it is said, identifying his own soil by its distinctive smell.

249

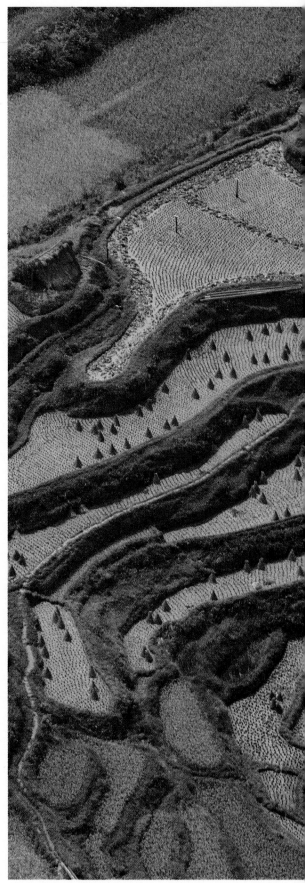

Millions of people in Asia depend on rice for survival. In southern China's Guizhou Province, stacked sheaves of rice dry in terraced paddies, awaiting threshing. To cultivate the steep terrain, farmers first sculpture terraces into the hillsides, following the contours of the land. Irrigation channels drain water from the top fields to flood the paddies.

Wearing a straw umbrella held on by a strap across her forehead, a farmer transplants rice shoots into a rain-dappled paddy in Nepal, outside Pokhara. The monsoon may bring an ample harvest or may send rivers spilling over their banks or mud slides careening down deforested slopes to ruin her family's fields and village.

Carefully tended terraces can last indefinitely. In the mountains of northern Luzon the Ifugao have farmed their terraced mountain slopes continuously for hundreds of years. There these industrious people transformed the steep slopes into rice fields that impressed one writer as "enormous gardens of fantastic beauty."

Still independent in their mountain fastness, the Ifugao prefer to be left alone. They cultivate rice on their terraces, and plots of sweet potatoes, beans, corn, peas, and cucumbers. Their small villages perch high in the mountains. But foreigners invade now in busloads—tourists who come to enjoy the cool green beauty of the mountains and to admire a system of rice terraces so extensive that their combined length equals approximately 12,000 miles—half the distance around the world.

Weaving, wood carving, basketry, and handicraft shops bolster the Ifugao economy by bringing in cash. A visitor watched an

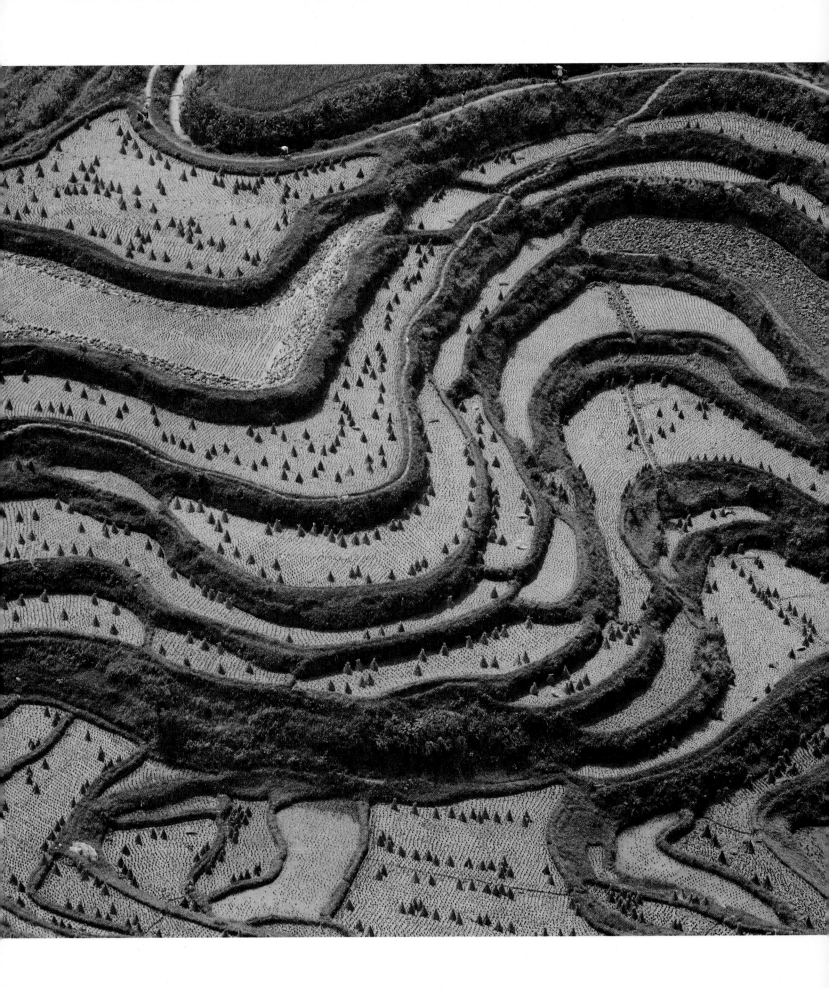

Ifugao woman weaving in a shop where the air was filled with lint from the yarn.

"How do you stand it?" the visitor asked.

"I work here for three days," she replied. "Then I must go and work in the rice terraces for a day, to get some fresh air."

In Papua New Guinea's central highlands live the Enga, a people whose existence the world little suspected before their discovery in the early 1930s by Australian mineral prospectors. The Enga live by a primitive agriculture focused on sweet potatoes and pigs. Before the outside world intruded, the Enga had no knowledge of metals. With tools and weapons made of wood and stone, they cut clearings in the dense forest, tilled the soil, and defended themselves. They had no villages. Men lived together in small clubhouses, while the women lived with the children and pigs in separate houses near the sweet potato gardens. Clothing was scanty; for warmth the Enga smeared their bodies with pig grease. Life was harsh. Many children died before the age of five.

Now, 50 years later, life for the Enga has changed. Steel tools have replaced stone.

Many Enga wear factory-made clothing from the outside world. There are roads and schools, and some of the young people speak English. A growing population finds land in short supply. But the basic method of cultivation has remained about the same.

The Enga live in a narrow strip of land that climbs from around 5,000 feet to 9,000 feet, a range of altitude at which their sweet potatoes can grow. At the lower end of this zone, crops mature in five to seven months; at the upper end, in twelve months. About half the sweet potatoes are used to feed the people, the rest to feed the pigs.

Frost is always a danger, especially at the higher levels, and the Enga have an ingenious method of coping with it. They construct circular mounds of dirt about ten feet across and two or three feet high, with a compost pile of dead vegetation in the middle. The potato vines are planted on top of the mounds. When the air freezes at night, the colder air sinks around the base of the mounds, keeping the tops warmer. The decomposing compost also adds a degree or two of warmth.

Nevertheless, severe frosts occur every ten to thirty years, destroying most of the potato plants. Enga tradition accommo-

Harvesting a contraband crop: In the hills of northern Thailand, people disregard risks to make money growing illegal opium. A woman scores opium poppy seed pods with a small knife to let sap ooze out and dry overnight into gummy raw opium. The opium poppy grows best in a cool highland climate. Since many of the workers are addicts, traders who buy the crop often pay in processed opium. Three or four times a day, an addict will heat opium and inhale the fumes that bring euphoria.

NEXT PAGE: In southern India's Nilgiri Hills, women pick tea by plucking only young leaves and buds. After some ten days they will harvest new growth.

253

254

dates these disasters. As common practice, the highland Enga present the valley Enga with pigs, bird plumes, and access to the upland pandanus groves, so that in times of crisis they can call in the debt and seek refuge below. Soon after moving into the valleys the highland Enga begin taking new potato plants back to their homes and replanting their gardens, knowing that it will take many months for the crops to mature.

But recent events have undermined this traditional pattern of self-reliance. After a series of killing frosts in 1972, hundreds of frightened people fled their ruined gardens, bringing along sheets of ice. They appeared at a missionary station. In pidgin they cried, "Everything is buggered up finish. Look at the ice."

The government helps, but the assistance weakens old ties between highland and valley Enga. Now the government has introduced cash crops—cabbage, carrots, and Irish potatoes. The Enga sell these in local markets, along with pandanus nuts, pigs, bird plumes, and animal skins, to earn money for manufactured goods. Sweet potatoes still form the bulk of the Enga diet but cash is now an integral part of the exchange system. Soon the valley people may ask for money instead of the traditional payment for their hospitality. It is hard for the Enga to earn much money. Many of the young people are now leaving home for jobs on coffee plantations.

Many mountain areas cannot be cultivated. In some of these places nomads use animals to harvest what little the land offers. Nomads have no permanent home; the word comes from the Greek for "one who wanders for pasture." In the spring, as the weather warms and grasses green, these pastoral nomads take their herds to higher altitudes. As winter approaches, they retreat to the lowlands, which have been watered by autumn rains. Uncountable numbers of people have followed this way of life for thousands of years. Even as late as 1950, nomads numbered 10 percent of the population of southwestern Asia—some five million people. Now estimates vary greatly from country to country: in Iran, perhaps 5 percent of the people, in Afghanistan possibly as many as 16 percent.

After a long trip for firewood, North Yemeni women trudge home to Manakbab, 7,500 feet up in the Jabal Haraz range. With few trees left amid stands of acacia scrub, soaring fuel costs and eroded slopes have led farmers to plant new trees.

Half of Nepal's forests have disappeared since the 1950s. Near Pokhara a young Nepalese woman plants bakena *seedlings. The fodder crop will help replace trees cleared for terraces, cut for firewood, or stripped of leaves for animal feed and bedding.*

257

In Guatemala's volcanic highlands, goats and sheep graze under the eyes of an Indian herder. The animals belong to several families, who consolidate their flocks so they may be tended by fewer people. The Indians also raise corn, using hoes and digging sticks much like those of their Maya ancestors. After harvesting the corn, farmers let herds forage on the stubble. Indians have farmed here for more than 7,000 years but have lost much of their land to plantations that grow coffee and other crops for export. On the small plots that remain, the Indians cannot raise enough food for their families, and most young children here suffer from malnutrition.

259

In the Andes sheep, cattle, alpacas, and llamas form the migratory herds; in Asia they are sheep, goats, cattle, and sometimes yaks, horses, and reindeer. The distances traveled by nomads between winter and summer pastures vary greatly from place to place. People of the Andes and the western Himalayas may travel only a few miles up and down river valleys, but in Iran the annual round-trip may be 600 miles.

Nomadism is a fading way of life. Nomads find less and less freedom. Where once they crossed open land, now they face irrigated fields, national boundaries, immigration laws, and other marks of settled populations. Governments declare nomadism to be anachronistic. They force nomads to abandon their ancient ways of life and to take up trades in which they have little skill or interest. This is especially true in the Himalayas and Tibet, where nomadic societies traditionally held high status, and working the soil was demeaning.

The Soviet Union gave up its attempts to change the Kirghiz, a people who for centuries have lived as nomads in the lofty Pamirs and Tian Shan of Central Asia. When cattle, goats, and sheep began starving on collective farms for lack of range, Soviet authorities decided that nomadism might after all be the most efficient way to exploit the mountain regions. By the 1960s Kirghiz families were again free to saddle their yaks and horses, and herd them to high summer pastures. There the families lived in yurts, comfortable in their old ways. When they followed the grass with their animals, they simply took apart the heavy felt coverings and wooden frames of the yurts, and moved their homes with the herds.

During the coldest months of winter, the Kirghiz return to the collectives, so they are not wandering nomads in the sense that their ancestors were. Roads, schools, and industry have come to the valleys of Kirghizia, and most of the animals are state property. But the Kirghiz retain the free spirit of an enduring mountain people, a spirit reflected in their old epic poem, "Like a wild mountain stream we ran down. . . . We flew like birds."

When American mountain climber and Soviet scholar William Garner talked with

Along the upper Ramu River in Papua New Guinea, Melanesian farmers have slashed and burned the rain forest on the slopes of the Bismarck Range to grow coffee and sugarcane.

Explorers following the Ramu in the 1920s and '30s discovered people as ignorant of the world as the world was of them. Isolated in highland valleys by jagged peaks, sheer cliffs, unnavigable rivers, and dense forests, the indigenous population had developed several hundred distinct groups, each with its own language and customs. Today, rough terrain continues to hamper communication, and some tribes may send messages via drumbeat or yodel.

261

the Kirghiz in 1985, they characterized their summers in the mountains as "real life," by far the best way for the children. Seeking the highest yurt he could find, Garner listened to a shepherd who, though aged, had been entrusted to care for his grandchildren for the summer. The world of this "mountain man" was isolated, yet so secure, that as far as he cared both America and Moscow might as well be on the moon. The old Kirghiz, said Garner, clearly saw himself as guardian also of the traditions of his people because to go to the mountains in the summertime is to say to the government that the Kirghiz are a free people.

Much more widespread than nomadism is a way of life known as transhumance. People who follow this way of life have modified the patterns of nomadism, but the origin of the name emphasizes how closely it links people and the land. Transhumance comes from the Latin *trans* and *humus,* across the earth. Only a few herders go with the livestock to their summer pastures in the highlands, while most of the people remain in villages or towns in the lowlands and raise the grain and hay that will feed the livestock during the winter.

In North America, transhumance cen-

tered in the mountains of the semiarid western United States. Those mountains have never been settled like the mountains of Europe and Asia but they were used for grazing. Thousands of the herders were Basque, brought over, chiefly in the early 1900s, by western ranchers from their homes in the Pyrenees, where transhumance was declining.

The mountain pasturelands were, for the most part, owned by the federal government, which charged a fee for the grazing. At the same time, however, it became apparent that the cattle and sheep—which naturalist John Muir called "hoofed locusts"—were damaging the alpine grasslands. Ecological awareness increased, along with the demand for more recreation areas. The ranchers, under land-use restrictions, began to depend more and more on fenced pastures and feedlots.

Today ranches may be long distances from the available mountain pastures. In Nevada and Utah, sheep are trucked as many as 300 miles between winter and summer pastures. Some 70,000 cattle are trucked each year between the southern Cascades in Oregon to the Sacramento Valley in California. One southern Idaho

Clans gather in Papua New Guinea to kill pigs in rituals honoring ancestors and celebrating the renewal of life. On a Simbu mountaintop, men club pigs to death and, to boost fertility, drain the blood onto roots to be planted later. After singeing hair off (opposite), the men carve the carcasses and layer the meat with moistened vegetables and banana leaves and hot rocks to steam in pits. Owners later hand out meat to repay debts and garner prestige. Guests gorge on the pork, a welcome change from the daily diet of sweet potatoes. Like this Mendi girl (above), some highlanders keep pigs as pets. The pets will be eaten, but seldom by the owners, who will give away the meat.

262

After three hours spent painting his face, a Huli man (opposite) in Papua New Guinea's Tari Valley joins clan members at a singsing before a pig kill. Dancers chant and bounce, setting feathers, fur, and other ornaments aquiver. Women sometimes wear paint, but men are peacocks in the Huli tribe. Sporting a wig made of human hair, another Huli primps for a social gathering in which marriageable adults look each other over. In the Simbu tradition, a similar occasion is known as a turnim-head ceremony.

A Tarahumara Indian seeks a little shade as he waits for Holy Week celebrations to begin. Mexico's Sierra Madre Occidental is a land of steep canyons and rugged plateaus where recesses sheltered Tarahumara ancestors from foreign intrusion. The daunting terrain limited visits by outsiders, although missionaries have made the journey since the 1600s and regularly tried to persuade or force the Indians to move into villages. The clerics made religious converts, but most Tarahumara live near their fields and hike into town for church services and fiestas.

rancher takes his sheep 900 miles from home to a winter range in California.

Many mountain people farm and herd. This life is celebrated in Johanna Spyri's classic *Heidi*. When Heidi and the young goatherd, Peter, first took the flocks to the Alpine pasture, the ground was "thickly covered with fragrant wild flowers. The whole air round was filled with the sweet odor.... The valley lay far below in the full morning sunshine. In front of her Heidi saw a great wide field of snow, stretching high up into the deep blue sky; on the left stood an enormous mass of rock, on each side of which a higher tower of bald, jagged cliffs rose into the sky.... The child sat as still as a mouse; everywhere there was a great, deep stillness; only the wind passed very softly and gently over the tender bluebells and the radiant golden rockroses."

In *Heidi* Johanna Spyri re-created scenes of her own girlhood home on a Swiss mountainside, overlooking a village, meadows, orchards, gardens, and hayfields, the classic Alps development of mixed farming and grazing. Ideally, each household must have access to land in several environments: high pastures, forest, meadow, and cultivated fields. The farmer who has fields at different elevations and settings can distribute his time and energy strategically throughout the seasons. The result is the storybook landscape of villages and patchwork fields, green valleys and snowy peaks.

Attitudes toward land use in the Alps have changed a great deal since World War II. New industries and a spectacular increase in tourism and the number of automobiles have transformed the mountain economy. Hotels, ski resorts, and summer cottages replace grainfields. Today, automobile traffic during holidays and weekends is often bumper to bumper. Land is now worth more as building sites than as farms. Today more people of the Alps work in tourism than full-time in agriculture.

Several years ago, realizing that the picturesque landscape was a major tourist attraction, the Alpine countries began paying subsidies to farmers to encourage them to stay and maintain production. Now, however, they emphasize the classic cultural landscape itself rather than the farming

267

The Tarahumara celebrate Holy Week with religious festivities and a three-day party. Blending Christianity and indigenous religion, these Indians worship Onorúame, a Christlike figure said to be fond of corn beer. Dressed up as Roman soldiers wielding wooden weapons, a Tarahumara band circles a village church. Young men coat themselves with paint or mud (left) and pretend to be devils, drinking too much corn beer and flirting with women. Many celebrants spend Easter Sunday recuperating.

A Tarahumara scoops a hewn wooden ball onto his toes, flinging it to a teammate in the semiannual kickball race between rival communities near Creel, Mexico. Stopping only to eat, drink, relieve themselves, or consult shamans, racers run five laps up and down the mountain in the 20-hour contest. Throughout the night, fans trot alongside, cheering and hoisting lanterns made of oversize tin cans. Competitors and spectators alike bet heavily on the outcome. Tarahumara, who begin jogging as soon as they can walk, call themselves Rarámuri, the foot runners. Masters of endurance, they traditionally hunted by chasing game for days, until their prey collapsed from exhaustion.

economy. Farmers can often buy grain or hay more cheaply from lowland sources than they can produce it on steep mountain slopes, but they must work their fields in order to receive the subsidy.

The villagers of Obergurgl in the Austrian Tyrol recently took steps to stabilize their town and the tourist industry. They decided to limit the building of new hotels, because they were afraid that more crowding would reduce the appeal of their village. Payments from the village coffers compensated those farmers who had planned to sell their land for development.

The Swiss have also devised strategies to make the high pastures profitable, and by some of these enterprises Swiss children can still enjoy the glory of the mountains as Heidi did. For example, villagers may pool their livestock and hire one or two families to spend the summer with the herd and to make cheese, a time-consuming chore done up on the slopes.

A few years ago I visited a village-owned Alpine meadow in western Switzerland. It lay at the head of a high valley backed by steep rock walls. Two families lived in a building that was part cabin, part barn, with no electricity. There was a narrow jeep trail, along which they transported new cheese wheels to the village co-op twice a week.

On this bright, beautiful afternoon, I was intrigued to find the 50 head of cattle bedded down in the barn. The explanation was that they had been milked in the morning, as usual, and, as usual, cheesemaking began soon afterward. If the cows had been turned out to graze during the day, the people would have had to milk again at night.

Although the Alps environment is largely being preserved, the same cannot be said of many other mountain areas, where rapid deforestation and erosion are destroying the landscape. Population growth and increased pressure on the land are chiefly to blame. People settle more and more marginal areas on steeper slopes and take fewer safeguards for preservation.

In the Himalayas, people are cutting trees and shrubs for firewood and animal fodder at a rate that far exceeds the rate at which the plants can replenish themselves. The onslaught of mountain trekkers and

271

tourists into countries such as Nepal raises the demand for wood. Woodcutting gives work to many people, but they must now cut smaller and smaller trees and transport them farther and farther.

Devastating landslides are common. In the space of just one morning in 1968, in the eastern Himalayas, 20,000 landslides tore up homes and rice fields, and killed 30,000 people. Rivers draining the Himalayas now carry some of the heaviest silt loads in the world. "Topsoil washing down into India and Bangladesh," wrote environmentalist Erik Eckholm, "is now Nepal's most precious export, but one for which it receives no compensation."

Population pressure was a problem against which many old, isolated mountain societies had developed safeguards. They set their own rules to protect their way of life, and to live successfully within the meager resources of their surroundings. In Norway and Switzerland in the late 18th century, local ordinances prohibited or delayed marriages when the population became too large. In some European mountains, custom sometimes defied law to pass land from generation to generation by primogeniture—only one child inherited, usually the oldest son. Other children, with no means of livelihood, lived in celibacy as nuns and priests or left home to join the military or to emigrate. Even today, in the Basque Pyrenees, so important is the in-

India's Darjeeling Railway, built a century ago to carry British civil servants and their families, still ferries travelers to Darjeeling, the cool hill station in sight of Everest and Kanchenjunga.

Near the Norwegian peak, Trolltindane, the Trolls' Path (opposite) follows a rugged old trail. The road carries skiers to the summer international slalom competitions at Trollstigheimen, where 20-foot snowbanks line the roadside—even in June.

NEXT PAGE: *In the Bolivian Andes, 21,201-foot Illimani crowns La Paz, at 12,000 feet Earth's highest city. The inhabitants produce extra red blood cells to draw more oxygen from the thin air.*

273

tegrity of centuries-old family homesteads that the custom of primogeniture has almost the force of law.

In the Himalayas of northwestern Nepal, ethnic Tibetans follow an age-old, rare form of marriage known as fraternal polyandry. Two, three, or more brothers share a wife in a single family. Thus, family fields and herds do not have to be divided, and there are husbands to go out with the herds and husbands to tend the crops. This type of marriage checks population because the women bear fewer babies—all the brothers are "father," and the "fathers" treat all the children equally. Fraternal polyandry is less common now because younger brothers can find work away from the farms and

Mineral riches are one bequest of mountain formation. At an open-pit mine in Australia's Hamersley Range, a shovel bites into one of the largest deposits of iron ore on Earth.

A steel mill on the Appalachian Plateau at Weirton, West Virginia, melts iron ore in blast furnaces where temperatures reach more than 3,000°F. Impurities rise to the top and are channeled into a train of slag ladles and towed to a storage dump. Later the slag is sold to be used for railroad ballast and road building.

277

prefer to have their own wives. These changes have fragmented families and their holdings. Attitudes towards land use are shifting from long-term conservation to short-term exploitation.

Both attitudes exist in the United States. Every year, more and more highland space is exploited for minerals or timber or turned to resort or housing development. Yet one soil conservation official in the Virginia Appalachians reports that "it's the newcomers, the retired people, who come to us for advice. Most of the farmers just keep cutting down more trees so that they can run more cattle. But they end up with no soil to grow grass."

In mountain regions throughout the world, it is increasingly difficult to protect conservative methods of land use. Roads penetrate isolated areas, bringing the more technical cultures of the lowlands. This is as it should be, if it means a more comfortable life for highlanders. But new ways are not necessarily better for the special requirements of mountain environments. When outsiders convince highlanders that the old ways are inferior, irreplaceable knowledge may be lost. Over the centuries, for instance, mountain people have developed special ways of making clothes and processing food. They have used tools suited to their fields—short-handled hoes and scythes, and implements that conserve their thin soil.

Highland people do not come with empty cups. They possess a wisdom that has been gained over centuries of cherishing the high places of the Earth. Robert Coles's young Appalachian friend knew well the source of their strength. "I do believe my people have been here so long," he said, "we'll never really leave, even if we do go to some city. . . . My daddy says, if he was in Dayton or Cleveland, and he was lying on his death bed, and ready to meet the Lord, the last thing he'd think of, before he would go to get judged, would be our hills—the sight of them, and the sky beyond, and the woods below, and our hollow and the whole length of the valley you can see from up there, on top of yonder mountain."

LARRY W. PRICE

Mountain sports exhilarate novice and champion athletes alike. Some 12,000 skiers glide across Lake Silvaplana in Switzerland's 26-mile Engadine Ski Marathon. Once purely a means of travel over snowbound land, cross-country skiing has become a popular pastime as people seek fitness and harmony with nature.

On the Owens Valley side of the Sierra Nevada, in California, a climber scales a 40-foot boulder. Using only his bare hands and special shoes that grip the rough surfaces, he focuses mind, body, and soul on each arduous move. On good days, his efforts repay him with a sense of spiritual unity with the mountains.

LIVING ON
COASTS

eyond many ocean horizons from where I am swimming off Zuma Beach in southern California, wind moves the ceiling of the sea into waves of liquid energy. They pass 13,000 feet above the floor of the Mendocino Fracture Zone and press eastward at a steady speed of 28 miles an hour. At the perimeter of the Pacific, they travel over the foot of our continent as it slopes upward from lightless depths toward sunbathed shallows.

Unimpeded by any boundary, the waves sweep into sovereign waters. On into the plankton-rich ocean edge, where abundant sea life is concentrated by sunlight, tides, and coastal upwelling. Through giant kelp forests and bobbing fishing boats with their gossamer skirts of monofilament set to catch dinner or to pay the mortgage. Over terrestrial debris dumped at sea.

As the continent rises beneath them, the waves change shape. A shoaling bottom drags and then trips them from below, and one by one they peak and topple.

Treading water on the outside edge of the breaking surf, I get ready to ride a seven-foot wave that stands like a green hill against the summer sky. As the swell walls up, I turn and swim hard with it until I catch its speed and turn and bodysurf across the thinning and towering face. It breaks and plunges me down with thousands of foot-pounds of energy, tumbling me over and over in sand-thick water until, exhausted and lungs bursting, I pop to the surface.

I marvel at the power and likely history of my wave. Judging from its size, it probably traveled far. Most of its short life was spent distant from people until in its last hours it traversed coastal waters, got a nationality, brushed against politics, ecology, and economics, and then in its final seconds picked up a hitchhiker and tons of sand and collapsed on Zuma Beach.

Thus Zuma pursues its annual cycle. Summer waves transport sand from offshore bars, and the beach builds up and out. In the winter, Pacific storms send large waves that cut the beach down and away, and redeposit offshore the accumulated summer sand. Each coast has its own rhythm composed of the changing seasonal convergence of land and sea patterns: wet and dry, tide and current, wind and calm, turbid and clear, and arrival and departure. Geographical location helps establish that rhythm on coasts of ice, rock, sand, coral, mud, or mangrove.

Where shallow waters lap over the continental shelves, the coasts provide access to the natural riches of both oceanic and terrestrial realms. The shelf waters swarm with sea life. Arctic and temperate waters have large numbers of a few marine species, while tropical coasts have small numbers of many species.

One such area is the northern coast of Australia. Aboriginal peoples have lived there for thousands of years and may well be the world's first coastal ecologists. Among them are the Yolngu of northeastern Arnhem Land in the Northern Territory, much of whose society, economy, and spiritual life focuses on their tropical coastline.

The Yolngu's ancestral territory embraces a 50-mile slice of coastal floodplains and river estuaries, with offshore mud flats, sandbanks, and waters that stretch 50 miles out to sea. Beyond the seaward horizon is "for the government." The people, around 5,000 in number, hunt, fish, and gather their food, which includes fish, shellfish, turtles and their eggs, and dugongs—sea mammals related to the manatees. In the interior the Yolngu seek wild nuts, roots, fruit, and honey, and hunt game such as wallabies, emus, and lizards.

The people live in central communities or associated outstations. At the outstations, traditional bough shelters mingle with modern houses—the latter usually made of fiberboard with corrugated metal roofs like those in the central communities. I visited one community of 20 or so homes, with an old Land-Rover drawn up in their midst. Rust red fuel drums dotted the area, the empties serving as rain barrels. The people wore light cotton clothing purchased in a nearby town. Outside the houses, families and visitors sat gossiping in the shade on mats woven from pandanus leaves. Socializing is an important activity and blurs the Western concept of distinct households. At night the kerosene lanterns hiss, illuminating groups visiting and telling stories.

Lifesaving beacons in fog or darkness, lighthouses guide mariners along Earth's coastlines. Here a fisherman tests his skill at dawn beside Brant Point Light at Nantucket harbor. Townsmen of this once prosperous whaling port voted funds for the first light here in 1746. Trading interests have erected lighthouses since antiquity at ports around the world.

Along with modern navigation aids, some 400 traditional light towers, now mostly automated, still beam their warning off the United States coasts.

PREVIOUS PAGE: Senegalese pirogues line the Atlantic surf at Kayar, which turns into a ghost village each year after a nine-month fishing season.

ARCTIC CIRCLE

North

Pacific

Ocean

Sitka
Ketchikan

*Puget
Sound*

N O R T H

*Penobscot
Bay*

A M E R I C A

San Francisco

*Nantucket
Island*

New York

*Chesapeake
Bay*

North

Atlantic

Ocean

Los Angeles

TROPIC OF CANCER

*Gulf of
Mexico*

EQUATOR   0°

S O U T H

Lima

A M E R I C A

TROPIC OF CAPRICORN

South

Pacific

Ocean

Shores of the Continents

*"Always the edge of the sea re-
mains an elusive and indefin-
able boundary," wrote
biologist Rachel Carson. Waves
shape and reshape coastlines,
sea level rises and falls. Geographers say Earth's coasts measure some 220,000 to 310,000
miles, but these figures rise dramatically if areas such as tidal
regions are included. The surrounding four oceans and
their seas are really one single
intermixing ocean that washes
over 70 percent of our planet's
surface with an average depth
of more than 12,000 feet.*

284

*Human and ocean life con-
centrate along the edges of
continents. Settlers or conquer-
ors often sailed in on the tide,
and towns sprang up around
likely harbors. Some, growing
into major ports, became the
world's largest cities. People living on coasts found continental shelves the most productive
areas of the sea. They yield 90
percent of the world's fish and
large amounts of oil, gas, and
minerals. Today, 200-nautical-
mile economic zones extend
national sovereignty over most
of these resources.*

Ocean

North
Sea
Oosterschelde
London   •Amsterdam
Cancale•   EUROPE
COSTA
BRAVA

ASIA

North

Pacific

Ocean

Mediterranean Sea

•Tokyo

Shanghai
Brahmaputra   Yangtze   East
Ganges   China
                                               Sea
AFRICA
•Kayar   Calcutta•
                          Bay
                          of
                          Bengal

INDONESIA
                                   Crocodile
                          Indian Ocean   Islands
                                   ARNHEM
                                   LAND

AUSTRALIA

South

Atlantic

Ocean

In the dry season, many people carry their household goods, pandanus mats, and fishing gear from the central communities to outstations or temporary camps along the coast. Here they settle into an age-old pattern of fishing and shellfish gathering. Ancient shell mounds on the beach, they say, are "from first time people, who lived from the sea as we do."

The Yolngu see themselves as guardians of a living coast. They believe that mythical ancestors created the coast and its plants and animals, transforming themselves into landforms—such as water holes, depressions, or hillocks—in the river mouths, estuaries, mangroves, and offshore shoals. To protect these sacred places and their food resources, the people follow elaborate rules. Strangers must seek permission to cross the Yolngu coast. Only the Yolngu may harvest food there, unless they invite other Aboriginal people to share a particularly abundant supply.

The Yolngu live within the seasonal rhythm of their coastal geography. The pace of life is set by tide and rain. Their land, a flat shelf, holds a shallow body of water that changes in depth with the tides, in extent with the rains, and in salinity with the seasons. From December to March the northwest monsoons bring rough winds and seas that prevent fishing, so the Yolngu gather shellfish from the mud flats and mangrove swamps.

One delicious meal I shared with Yolngu hosts was large-clawed mud crabs, three or four pounds in weight, boiled in seawater right on the beach next to the mangrove where they were caught. The crabs come out of their holes as the tide goes out. They can be caught by hand, but not easily held. The men go after them with spears and *whap!* into a woven pandanus bag, then another, *whap!* Children, too, delight in pitting themselves against a mud crab. People crack them open with heavy sticks, as there are few rocks along this coast.

In April the winds begin to shift to the southeast and come dry from the land. The coastal and floodplain waters grow calm. The men travel by bark canoe or aluminum dinghy to the edge of their world—to the Crocodile Islands and other offshore

islands—to harpoon the 300-pound green turtles, and dugongs that range from 700 to 900 pounds. And they spread out across the inundated waterscape to spear giant perch called barramundi.

In shallows just above my knees, I stand with a Yolngu friend, Frank Gulpalil, waiting for a distant fish wake to approach. We have waded offshore to where fish feed on the rising tide. "Everything moves on the tide," says Gulpalil. He shows me how each wake telegraphs a fish's species, size, and depth. This one indicates a barramundi, probably 15 pounds. Gulpalil holds a bamboo fish spear with three metal prongs.

The fish wake cruises slowly forward, moving in the long S-curves that mark a

Coastal fishermen of southeast Alaska owe their sea harvests to regulations that maintain the supply. A worker in a Ketchikan packinghouse (above) ices down a fine catch of halibut, largest of all the flatfish, after a season limited to five days. On a tender off Sitka, a silvery cascade of herring (opposite) represents one crew's share of a frenzied four-hour season that was valued at four million dollars. The high price comes from the roe—exported as a delicacy to Japan, whose own herring grounds are fished out.

287

barramundi. Gulpalil judges its speed and depth and throws his spear sidearmed and low, so that it cuts the surface at an angle and hits the fish behind its gills. The barramundi flashes and splashes in the shallows, but the spear won't pull out.

We take our catch home to Gulpalil's wife, who roasts it over a wood fire. We eat the succulent white fillets, together with shellfish that pop open in the heat from the embers, and hot bread baked in the ashes.

The Yolngu catch barramundi only at special times and places. They do not fish them in the river mouths and estuaries, because these are sacred places and also important barramundi migration corridors. By restricting entry, the Yolngu protect the estuaries—among the most productive yet fragile of all coastal ecosystems.

Commercial fishermen of the 1970s came into conflict with the Yolngu. The fishermen regarded the barramundi and coastal waters as Australian resources open to all Australians. Some even set nets in the river mouths and estuaries after the practice was outlawed in 1980. A lucrative commercial catch, barramundi bring more than two million dollars a year in sales in the Northern Territory.

The Yolngu took their complaint to court in Darwin, seat of the Northern Territory government. In 1983 the court recognized Yolngu rights in Castlereagh Bay to coastal waters within one and a quarter miles of the mainland and of the Crocodile Islands. The case had a welcome postscript: Studies conducted in the 1980s demonstrated the Yolngu's superior knowledge of barramundi habits. These days, commercial fishermen are cooperating with the Yolngu in conserving this joint resource.

The Yolngu won this case, but sometimes modern laws change the lives of native coastal societies. The Inuit and North American Indians living on the icy shores of Canada and Alaska have lost most of their traditional territories and the unrestricted freedom to hunt seals and whales as their forefathers did. Many now hold paying jobs.

And the Lummi of Puget Sound in the Pacific Northwest are locked in combat with the United States Internal Revenue Service over taxes on their salmon catch. By treaty, they assert, they are a distinct nation exploiting their own natural resources. Japanese fleets net American salmon in the North Pacific, they say, so why not tax Japan? Some Lummi have burned fishing boats to

"The immense protein factory," journalist H.L. Mencken called Chesapeake Bay for its seafood. A bay oysterman (opposite) hauls a dredgeful aboard the skipjack Maggie Lee, *one of the nation's last working sailboats. Cost-return ratios may soon put the vintage skipjacks out of business. Disease and pollution—and, some say, overfishing—have halved oyster crops.*

A diner (above) prepares to enjoy her choice of seafood: a Maine lobster. And mussels, European favorites, grow in a sea farm at Cancale, France. In the 13th century, a shipwrecked Irish sailor found that mussels grew abundantly on the poles of a net he had strung to catch seabirds. Poles are used in much the same way to this day.

289

Lobsters, arduously trapped in wire or wooden cages, tempt gourmet palates from Maine to Australia. Their popularity and scarcity keep prices high.

A rock lobster (left) dangles in a wire-mesh pot off Australia's southern coast. It will soon be hauled up and jetted live to an Australian or Far Eastern market—or sold as frozen lobster-tail, probably in the United States. Rock lobsters differ from American lobsters in having slender claws—a crucial difference for Maine lobster lovers, who relish large claws full of tender meat.

In Maine many lobstermen are switching to wire traps. Rectangular in shape, they weigh less and last longer than traditional oak traps, such as those piled (above) on a dock at Bernard. Nylon lines, Styrofoam buoys, fiberglass hulls, and electronic gear are also modernizing a lobsterman's tools, but he must still take his chances with thick fog, storms, and frigid waters. So risky is lobstering that insurance companies rate it on a par with steeplejacking or coal mining.

291

prevent them being seized for back taxes. Meantime, white fishermen complain bitterly about the Lummi's privileged status, which guarantees them, along with other American Indians of the Pacific Northwest, the first 50 percent of the salmon catch.

Fishing disputes over coastal access and resources remain commonplace in many countries, but informal rights to fishing territories often resolve them. Maine's lobster boats, their engine beats magnified in the silent dawn, chug out to their owners' recognized territories, dotted with the distinctive colors of their lobster buoys. Groups out of the same harbor work areas of about a hundred square miles, a tradition established in the late 1800s.

On Maine's rocky coast, whose drowned mountains crest above the waters as offshore islands, the sea is the chief resource. Ice Age glaciers scraped away much of the soil, leaving a thin layer where scrub, blueberry bushes, and pointed fir trees grow—and little else. In 1614 English explorer Capt. John Smith wrote "as farre as I could see Eastward . . . is nothing but such high craggy Cliffy rocks and stony Iles, that I wondered such great trees could growe upon so hard foundation."

Generations of Maine coast dwellers chopped down those trees to build their clapboard or shingle homes and wooden boats. Many people, particularly Down East in the Penobscot Bay region, still travel by boat from one of Maine's 3,000 "stony Iles" in the summer season to pick up mail, groceries, or visitors from the mainland.

In the 1800s small Penobscot Bay island communities existed year-round. Islanders quarried the granite bedrock, tended lighthouses, farmed vegetable patches, and opened the first boardinghouses for "summer rusticators." Their children attended class in one-room schoolhouses, such as the one preserved intact on Eagle Island. No pupils sit at those desks any more. With the advent of railroads, the advantages of Maine's watery highways disappeared, and islanders moved to the mainland. Most of these islands have turned into summer

292

Mobile-home owners of Pacifica, California (left), experienced the hazards of coastal life in March 1983. Pounding storm surf destroyed their seawall and lapped at their doors. Experts increasingly blame such damage on man-made barriers that undermine the coast's natural defenses. Waves rebound sharply from seawalls, washing away sandy beaches that once cushioned the waves' impact. Groins such as those (above) at Sandy Hook, New Jersey, trap sand, but deprive other beaches down the coast.

293

retreats for local people or outsiders, remote from tourists on the mainland dreaming of Maine lobsters.

To make that dream come true, sweatered, booted lobstermen ready their boats on summer mornings for the daily lobster run. An average boat, some 35 feet long, has a high bow and squared-off wheelhouse opening back into a spacious cockpit. The captain steers for the bobbing specks of color that mark his lobster traps—also called pots. He swings his boat's starboard side up to each buoy and lifts his traps, usually with a mechanical pot hauler. Discarding unwanted fish and debris, he measures lobsters with a size gauge that tells him which, by state law, are "keepers" and which are too small and must be thrown back. "Berried" females—ones bearing eggs—get their tails notched and go back to renew the stock.

Despite such regulations, the lobster haul is declining. Lobstermen now set three times as many traps as in the 1960s to get the same return. Environmentalists talk of pollution, but lobstermen say the problem is overfishing. It is not theirs alone.

In the 1950s continental-shelf fishing intensified through the use of better and bigger boats and improved technology. The large catches of schooling fish, such as anchovies, herring, and menhaden, appeared to justify greater exploitation. Global fishing yields increased by 8 percent annually. But by the 1960s and '70s, yields were declining worldwide—an alarming trend that has led to conservation measures.

Peruvians have fished their 1,400-mile coastline for at least a thousand years. In this land of little rainfall, the arid sands preserve signs of large pre-Inca civilizations that flourished here by fishing and by farming the fertile river valleys. Modern farmers irrigate these same desert lands to produce major crops of sugar and cotton. Others grow grapes near Pisco—which gives its name to a local wine-brandy—or the fiery orange peppers that flavor Peruvian dishes.

The dry climate provides perfect beach weather for the inhabitants of Peru's half-modern, half-Spanish colonial capital, Lima. Families flock on weekends to resorts such as Ancón, (Continued on page 301)

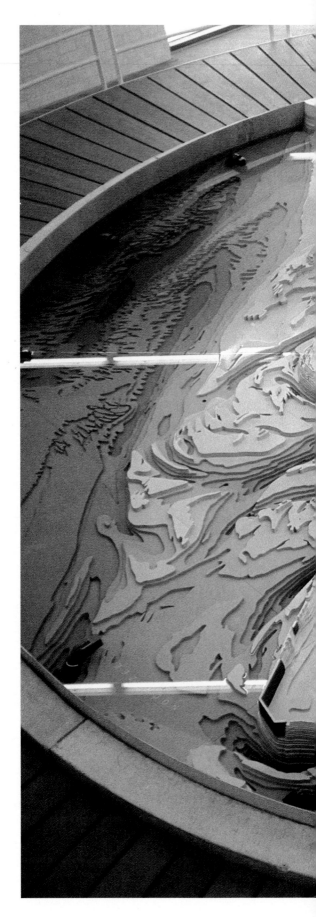

Workers examine a model of the Dutch Delta Project's sea defenses. Designed to be flooded with water, the model shows where North Sea storm waters would surge without the system of dams and dikes.

More than half the population of the Netherlands lives on coastal lowlands threatened by the sea. In 1953, when storm floods killed 1,800 people, the government said "never again" and began the five-billion-dollar Delta Project. Its most ambitious feature, shown at center as a yellow, boxy structure, is a mammoth storm-surge barrier that will seal the mouth of the Oosterschelde— the eastern arm of the River Schelde's estuary—when storms strike again.

Mattressing filled with sand and gravel (left) winds onto a giant drum for transportation to the site of the Dutch Oosterschelde barrier. When laid on the sandy estuary floor, it will prevent erosion and provide a stable foundation for the barrier's 66 concrete piers.

The final stage of the Delta Project, the barrier was originally planned as a solid dam. Environmentalists protested that this would destroy the estuary's tidal ecology, including its rich harvests of mussels and oysters. To avoid this, the completed barrier's gates remain open during normal tidal flow (right) but can be lowered within an hour. A similar barrier on the Thames protects London from tidal surges.

298

Wind power has reinforced Dutch manpower since the 17th century to pump water from much needed land. Nearly half of the densely populated Netherlands consists of reclaimed lands called polders that once were inland lakes or coastal marshes. Polders have reclaimed some 400,000 acres of the former Zuiderzee, now a dam-sealed lake, IJsselmeer, where boats float (above).

Polder mills, such as this one at Stompetoren near Amsterdam, help drain the land. The miller (left) operates the gears that turn the top of the windmill into the wind. Then he unfurls and adjusts the sails (opposite). Today steam, diesel, and electric pumps have replaced most polder mills.

a former fishing village, where skyscraper apartment buildings now tower over the fishermen's homes.

The waters off this dry coast contain some of the greatest concentrations of marine life in the world. The cool Peru Current combines with the upwelling of cold, nutrient-bearing waters to encourage a prolific growth of plankton, and fish thrive on it. Peru once hauled a startling 20 percent of the world's fish catch from this thin slice of coastal waters. The most valuable part, yielding a third of the country's export revenue in 1970, was the anchovy catch, much of which was converted to fish meal.

The anchovies also feed millions of seabirds, which nest on islands off the coast. Their droppings have accumulated in pungent layers up to 150 feet thick because of the lack of rain. Laboring in the stench and dust, Peruvian workers scrape up this guano. It was widely used as fertilizer before the day of chemical fertilizers.

Peru suffers an occasional climatic upheaval that forms part of a fluctuation in ocean-atmospheric relations in the equatorial Pacific. Torrential rainstorms wash out normally arid communities, while drought may strike areas from Mexico to Australia.

Called El Niño ("the Christ child") in Peru because it often occurs around Christmas, it causes massive fish kills. Warm equatorial waters move south, displacing the Peru Current and reducing upwelling. Without a nutrient supply, the plankton thins out, fish disappear, and seabirds starve. Tons of rotting fish litter beaches, exuding gases that are said to discolor and blister paint on boats—an occurrence Peruvians call El Pintor, "the painter."

One of Peru's main fishing communities is Callao, also the port for Lima. When I visited Callao in the mid-1970s, the fishermen were experiencing a drastic decline in their harvests and blaming El Niño of 1972-73. A double row of rusty trawlers lay idle, tied bow to stern. Jorge Sánchez, an unemployed deckhand, explained, "There's no work. We are fishermen without fish." But he was philosophical about it. The fish must have gone somewhere else. In an El Niño year, the fishing is bad. Later, in a non-El Niño year, they come back.

Rescued from drowning, farm polder land in the Netherlands is hedged by drainage ditches that control flooding. The Dutch must stay on constant guard to keep the land they have wrested from the clutches of the sea. So much land is man-made in the Dutch coastal provinces of North and South Holland that the saying goes, "God made the world, but the Dutch made Holland."

NEXT PAGE: New York's East River, a passageway for shipping, serves as a reminder that the city owes its origin and fortunes to its coastal location. Its sheltered anchorage makes it one of the world's great port cities and gateway to a nation.

301

But Sánchez saw himself in a cycle that no longer existed. Probably due to a combination of El Niño and overfishing, the fish did not come back in sizable numbers by 1977, and the anchovy fishery nearly collapsed. Fishermen lost their jobs and boats, and fish-meal plants closed down. Belated restrictions have somewhat revived the anchovy stocks, but many fishermen and plant workers have had to find other work in the port of Callao.

As weather can help destroy the livelihood of coastal dwellers, it can also threaten their very lives. One of the world's most hazardous coasts belongs to Bangladesh. The eighth most populous country on Earth, Bangladesh has more than 107 million people crammed into an area smaller than Wisconsin, whose population is 4.7 million. Land pressure is pushing people off the mainland onto temporary mud islands barely above sea level.

The country is basically made up of sediment. The Ganges and Brahmaputra Rivers carry a combined 2.4 billion tons of sediment annually to their confluence from huge watersheds reaching north of the Himalayas. The rivers deposit the sediment as they flow more slowly through the delta into coastal waters, forming countless soft mud-and-silt islands known as *chars*.

Among the chars, maps are meaningless. Almost awash in the delta waters, the islands represent new land for landless people. Millions live on them. Families search continually for new chars that may appear overnight. New islands are too soupy to live on the first year, so squatters bring cattle, goats, and other animals to mark their claim and to pack down the silt. "The waters bring us land," char dwellers told me, "but next year all this could be gone."

If the char holds through the next rainy season, the people plant trees and bushes to anchor it against the currents, and move into houses woven from rushes to cultivate patches of rice and vegetables. The delta waters are filled with chars and their tiny communities struggling against poverty and nature. They have no government or

A solitary junk threads its way between barges and ferry in China's busiest port—Shanghai. The city's name, which means "up from the sea," encapsulates its history. Once a sleepy fishing village, Shanghai began to grow in the 13th century after silt from the Yangtze River shut down Suzhou, the port that had dominated Chinese trade. Shanghai, strategically situated between the Yangtze and the East China Sea on the Huangpu waterway, links the outer world and the Yangtze, the main avenue for China's internal cargo traffic. Some 100 million tons of goods pass through this city's waterfront each year, accounting for more than a fourth of the nation's foreign commerce.

police, no schools or doctors. Fierce battles break out between char dwellers and local strong men over possession of the islands and their meager crops and livestock. Cargo and fishing boats ply the choppy brown waters, lacing together the tough char people and their precarious livelihood.

The northeastern Indian Ocean and Bay of Bengal are breeding grounds for cyclones, many of which slam into the Bangladesh coast and the chars. In November 1970 a cyclone drove a 20-foot-high wall of water through the delta, killing half a million to a million people. Flooding brings further disaster almost every year.

To protect cropland on part of the coast, the government hired Dutch engineers to dam the Feni River mouth at the head of the Bay of Bengal. In 1985 an army of Bengali workers under Dutch and Japanese supervision built a dam more than half a mile wide on a base of mattressing topped with rocks, bags of clay, and kiln-baked bricks. It encloses, Netherlands-style, a large farming and reservoir area. When the next cyclone came, the dam held.

Dutch engineers have plenty of experience in building coastal barriers. The history and geography of the Netherlands are intimately tied to coastal flooding and engineering attempts to stem a sea that has for centuries claimed a massive toll of human life. Severe North Sea storm winds and rains combine with abnormally high tides to produce floodwaters that periodically sweep across these flat lowlands.

The inhabitants fought flood problems in prehistoric times by living on artificial mounds. In the ninth century A.D. they built the first seawalls, which were maintained by law. "Dike or depart" was the rule. In spite of these efforts, more than 130 major floods have wracked the country since A.D. 1000. In 1287 the sea rushed in, killing 50,000 people and helping to form a huge inland sea, the Zuiderzee. Over the succeeding centuries the Dutch installed a whole system of dikes and seawalls.

Modern Dutch sea defenses total 1,200 miles. Behind them, the people have reclaimed marshes and lakes with windmill pumps, creating their fertile landscape threaded with canals and drainage ditches. About 60 percent of the present population of 14.6 million lives on lands that would be covered by the sea without the system of dikes and dams. Even the capital of Amsterdam, with its 17th-century houses and

307

modern apartment blocks, its churches and discos, its staid burghers and drug-culture dropouts, lies below sea level. Some 3,000 families live in houseboats on its canals.

Ready access to the sea and keen trading skills enabled the Dutch, along with other European powers, to ferry commerce and conquest around the world. Maritime might carried the Dutch, Spanish, Portuguese, French, and British across the oceans to distant coasts where they built colonial empires, imposed new languages and religions and governments, and exported the local resources—from spices to slaves. They established coastal trading and garrison towns that grew into major ports.

Access to sea transportation has long influenced human settlement. Ancient and modern villages and cities have clung to and grown on coasts. Many of the world's largest cities have direct or river-borne access to the coast, from Tokyo and New York to London, Calcutta, and Shanghai.

Opened by British military force to foreign commerce in 1843 after the Opium Wars, Shanghai is China's largest, most cosmopolitan city, with some 12 million inhabitants. Most foreign trade and influence has come to China through Shanghai. The people have acquired business acumen and a spirit of adventure from their contacts with the outside world. Shanghai remains the country's major port and center of industry, research, and culture.

Cleaned up by the Communists, the city no longer teems with brothels and bars from which drunks could be "shanghaied" aboard a departing ship. Today, sailors on shore leave may be offered tickets to operatic and acrobatic performances or visits to the zoo by a seamen's club in the former British consulate on the waterfront. Beneath its windows, coastal and foreign ships hoot and jostle through the Huangpu waterway—Shanghai's link with the sea that brought commerce to its doors.

Since World War II decolonization has swept away most foreign control of distant cities and coasts. But a recent treaty recognizes new territories along the world's

"Beauty Lives In Hard Times," proclaims a Shanghai advertisement for Gone With The Wind. *The city's avid moviegoers will stand in line all day for scarce tickets, especially for a foreign film. Since European traders took over the port in the mid-1800s, Shanghai has been China's trendiest city, one that embraces all manner of foreign influence. Here, in the shadow of European-style mansions and grand hotels, prostitution and opium dens once flourished, along with major banking houses, a racetrack, and all-night bars. No alien idea was too bold, including the one that prompted a handful of intellectuals to form the Chinese Communist Party here in 1921.*

coastlines: the 1982 United Nations Law of the Sea. It has set off a mammoth 20th-century "ocean rush." Countries with coasts, either island or mainland, are exploring the resources of 200-nautical-mile Exclusive Economic Zones. For the United States—which made its claim independently—this new frontier region equals in importance the Louisiana Purchase of 1803. It doubles the nation's territory and raises fresh questions about resource conservation and coastal protection.

No coastline is stable. All change their shape and location over time because of erosion by wind, wave, sand, and water. Beaches, like Zuma Beach in California, are the coastal features that change most visibly season to season and year to year, owing to much the same environmental forces that more slowly re-form whole continental outlines. But people, adding their impact to nature's, are exerting increasing pressure on coasts, often with devastating results.

Sun coasts draw people like magnets. Every summer, tourism sets in motion temporary migrations of millions of people. Beaches from Spain's Costa Brava to California's Malibu are filled with people sunning, surfing, swimming, sailing, and playing. In the winter, beach visitors are few and different: Lone joggers in hooded sweatsuits run large dogs; a few young couples walk arm in arm along the high-water foam line; a retired couple with a new camper sips hot coffee from a thermos.

Besides vacationing there, many Americans are moving toward the coast. Already more than half the United States population lives within 50 miles of it. Some families buy or build homes right on the beach. Construction and human traffic harm sand dunes and barrier islands that once buffered coasts against storms. So do dredging and clearing to form new beaches and bays, and building seawalls.

With its steep, resistant surface, a seawall usually increases wave impact instead of dissipating it as a sandy slope does. After the violent West Coast storms of 1983, I went to look at the damage in Pacifica, south of San Francisco. There the surf had crashed over a seawall, undercut a road, and poured into the houses. People were

310

Tradition and modernity thrive side by side in Shanghai, known throughout China for its sophisticated sense of style. Models (above) display daring fashions for the new season at a local silk factory, while workers in traditional garb (left) line up to enter a restaurant. The same city that opened the first disco for foreigners and spawned student movements in recent years also lovingly preserves Buddhist temples, archaeological treasures, and ancient art objects that trace China's long history.

311

mopping up. Portable pumps thumped away, their hoses crisscrossing in all directions. Twenty-foot waves still swept over an L-shaped pier, where families used to stroll.

But on sandy Stinson Beach to the north, householders had fared no better. Their beach, scoured of its sand by winter storms, no longer formed an effective buffer. It had disappeared, and piles of sand lay in front rooms. Since then, the owners have built sturdy wooden barriers to seaward—but only about four feet high, so as not to obstruct the ocean view.

Recognizing the threat of rising sea level—a foot in the last century—and the inevitability of some erosion, most American states now restrict coastal development and invest in programs to stem further damage. But the quandary remains that homeowners, backed up by the protection of federal flood insurance, are reluctant to abandon their beautiful, high-risk locations.

The greater number of people living on or near coasts has meant that more sewage, farm fertilizers, and industrial wastes enter the water. Swimmers on the East Coast have been warned of fecal bacteria, and there is growing concern over food poisoning from eating raw clams, mussels, or oysters.

Nutrients in these wastes may trigger the explosive growth of algae, causing red or brown tides and depleting dissolved oxygen in the water—a serious threat to seafood supplies. Lobsters have suffocated in their traps in Long Island Sound. And the Chesapeake Bay oyster harvest has plummeted over the past decade, jeopardizing the livelihood of whole fishing communities. State governments in the bay area are now collaborating on a plan to reduce nutrients by 40 percent by the year 2000.

Along the narrow strips of low land and shallow waters that make up the Earth's coasts live the majority of the world's people and the greatest diversity of the ocean's organisms. The juxtaposition of land and sea concentrates life and now life's problems. From here, facing the waves, we will see the ocean breach and flood the land, and we will witness the loss of fish and other food resources from coastal waters, unless we can still learn, like the Yolngu, to respect our living coast.

BERNARD NIETSCHMANN

Relaxing on beach towels or frolicking in the warm Mediterranean, a crush of vacationers seek sun and fun on Spain's Costa Brava. Its mild climate, sandy coves, and rugged beauty attract visitors year-round.

Early seafarers—Phoenicians, Greeks, and Romans—built trading ports in sheltered harbors along this shore. Later, armies of Goths and Moors swept through. Down the ages, farmers on the coast grew grapes and olives, and fishermen hauled in their catches.

Today, former fishing villages sprout high-rise hotels, making Costa Brava one of Europe's top holiday coasts. Tourists, here and worldwide, have added a new chapter to living on Earth's coasts.

ILLUSTRATIONS CREDITS

The following abbreviations are used in this list: (t)-top; (b)-bottom; (r)-right; (l)-left; NGP-National Geographic Photographer; NGS-National Geographic Staff.

Pages 2-3, David Robert Austen.

Living in Arid Lands
12-13, Michael and Aubine Kirtley. 15, Rick Smolan, Contact Stock/Woodfin Camp. 19, Victor Englebert. 20-21, Kevin Fleming. 21(r), Carol Beckwith, from *Nomads of Niger*, published by Harry N. Abrams, Inc., 1983. 22-23, Dr. Hans Ritter. 24, Victor Englebert. 26-27, Kevin Fleming. 28(l), Erich Lessing, Magnum. 28(r), Michael Yamashita, Woodfin Camp. 29, Robert Azzi, Woodfin Camp. 30-31, Steve McCurry. 32, Georg Gerster, Zumikon, Switzerland. 33, Kevin Fleming. 34-35, Roland and Sabrina Michaud. 36, Kevin Fleming. 37, Carol Beckwith, from *Nomads of Niger*, published by Harry N. Abrams, Inc., 1983. 39, Wayne Eastep. 40(l), Kevin Fleming. 40-41, Raghubir Singh. 42-43, Georg Gerster, Zumikon, Switzerland. 43(r), Carol Beckwith, from *Nomads of Niger*, published by Harry N. Abrams, Inc., 1983. 44-45, Steve McCurry. 46, James L. Stanfield, NGP. 47, Georg Gerster, Zumikon, Switzerland. 48-49, Nathan Benn. 50(l), H. Edward Kim. 50-51, 52-53, Craig Aurness, West Light.

Living in the Arctic
54-57, Bryan and Cherry Alexander. 60-61, Fred Bruemmer. 62, Bryan and Cherry Alexander. 63(l), Yva Momatiuk and John Eastcott, Woodfin Camp. 63(r), Fred Bruemmer. 64-65, 66-67(t), Bryan and Cherry Alexander. 66-67(b), 67(br), 68-69, Michael St. Maur Sheil, Susan Griggs Agency. 70, James Balog. 71, Victor R. Boswell, NGP. 72-73, Bryan and Cherry Alexander. 74-77(rt), James Balog. 77(rb), Bryan and Cherry Alexander. 78, Dean Conger, NGS. 79, Bryan and Cherry Alexander. 80-83, James Balog. 84-85, Steve McCutcheon, Alaska Pictorial Service.

Living on Islands
86-87, Frans Lanting. 89, Steve McCurry. 92-93, Kristján Magnússon. 94-95, Frans Lanting. 96(lt), James P. Blair, NGP. 96(lb), 97, Frans Lanting. 98-99, Nicholas DeVore III, Photographers/Aspen. 100-101, Frans Lanting.

102-103, David Robert Austen. 103(r), Frans Lanting. 104(l), David Robert Austen. 104-105, Melinda Berge, Photographers/Aspen. 106, John Scofield. 107, David Robert Austen. 108-109, Steve McCurry. 110-111, Frans Lanting. 112, Raghubir Singh. 114-115, Hans J. Burkard, Bilderberg Archiv der Fotografen. 116, Carl Mydans, Black Star. 117, Melinda Berge, Photographers/Aspen. 118-119, Georg Gerster, Zumikon, Switzerland. 119(r), Wayne Eastep. 120-121, Fred Ward. 122-123, Chris Johns. 124, Steve Raymer, NGP. 125, Jodi Cobb, NGP.

Living with Forests
126-127, Alberto Venzago, Magnum. 129, 132-133(l), Jose Azel. 133(r), 134(l), Alberto Venzago, Magnum. 134-135, Miguel Rio Branco, Magnum. 136-137, Jose Azel. 137(rt, rb), Frans Lanting. 138-141, Jose Azel. 142-143, Alberto Venzago, Magnum. 144-151, Jose Azel. 152-153, Tony Morrison, South American Pictures. 153(r), Edward Parker, South American Pictures. 154(l), David Alan Harvey. 154-155, North Sullivan, Susan Griggs Agency. 156, Chris Johns. 157, William R. Sallaz, Black Star. 158-159, Gerald Frederick, Paula Crane's Faces/Places Photo Agency. 160-161, Chris Johns. 161(r), Joel Rogers, Earth Images. 162(lt), Terry Domico, Earth Images. 162(lb), 162-163, Chris Johns.

Living on Grasslands
164-165, Farrell Grehan. 167, Ottmar Bierwagen, Black Star. 170-171, Robert Caputo. 172-175(l), Carol Beckwith, from *Maasai*, published by Harry N. Abrams, Inc., 1980. 175(r), Robert Caputo. 176-177, Carol Beckwith, from *Maasai*, published by Harry N. Abrams, Inc., 1980. 178-179, Margaret Courtney-Clarke. 180-181, O. Louis Mazzatenta, NGS. 182-185, Steve Raymer, NGP. 186-187, Annie Griffiths. 188(l), Sam Chase. 188-189, Annie Griffiths. 190-191, George Olson. 192-193, Joel Rogers, Earth Images. 193(r), Annie Griffiths. 194-195, Ottmar Bierwagen, Black Star.

Living by Rivers
196-197, Raghubir Singh. 199, Enrico Ferorelli, Dot Photo Agency. 202, Stephanie Maze. 203, Loren McIntyre. 204-205, Hiroji Kubota, Magnum. 206-207, Jonathan Wright. 207(r), Georg Gerster, Zumikon, Switzerland. 209,

Steve McCurry. 210-211, Seny Norasingh. 212, Paul C. Pet, Amsterdam, the Netherlands. 213, Seny Norasingh. 214-215, Steve McCurry. 216-217, Raghubir Singh. 217(r) Seny Norasingh. 218-219, Raghubir Singh. 220, Paul C. Pet, Amsterdam, the Netherlands. 222(lt), Steve McCurry, Magnum. 222(lb), Anthony Bannister. 222-223, David Robert Austen, Woodfin Camp. 224(b), R. Ian Lloyd, Singapore. 224-225, Robert Caputo. 226-227, John de Visser. 228-229, David Hiser, Photographers/Aspen. 229(r), Dewitt Jones. 230(l), Bryan and Cherry Alexander. 230(r)-235, Adam Woolfitt, Susan Griggs Agency.

Living in Highlands
236-237, Thomas J. Abercrombie, NGS. 239, Paul C. Pet, Amsterdam, the Netherlands. 242, David Hiser, Photographers/Aspen. 243, Gilles Peress, Magnum. 244-247, Ken Heyman. 248-249, Pierre Boulat. 250(l), Steve McCurry. 250-251, Georg Gerster, Zumikon, Switzerland. 252-253, Seny Norasingh. 254-256, Paul C. Pet, Amsterdam, the Netherlands. 257, Steve McCurry. 258-259, Paul C. Pet, Amsterdam, the Netherlands. 260-261, David Robert Austen. 262(l), Ken Heyman. 262(r), 263, Danny Lehman. 264-265, Ken Heyman. 266-267, 268(l), Gilles Peress, Magnum. 268(r), John Running. 269-271, Gilles Peress, Magnum. 272-273, Paul C. Pet, Amsterdam, the Netherlands. 274-275, Loren McIntyre. 276-277, James A. Sugar, Black Star. 277(r), Jodi Cobb, Woodfin Camp. 278, Galen Rowell, Mountain Light. 279, Cotton Coulson, Woodfin Camp.

Living on Coasts
280-281, Georg Gerster, Zumikon, Switzerland. 283, David Alan Harvey. 286, Terry Domico, Earth Images. 287, William E. Thompson. 288, Emory Kristof, NGP. 289(l), Robert E. Gilka. 289(r), Bryan and Cherry Alexander. 290-291, David Doubilet. 291, Dwight R. Kuhn, DRK Photo. 292-293, James A. Sugar, Black Star. 293(r), David Alan Harvey. 294-295, Patrick Ward. 296-297(l), Farrell Grehan. 297(r)-299, Patrick Ward. 300-301, Farrell Grehan. 302-303, Jak Rajs, Image Bank. 304-305, Bruce Dale, NGP. 306-311, Jodi Cobb, NGP. 312-313, Stephanie Maze.

BIBLIOGRAPHY

We found the following books to be particularly helpful.

General sources include Bernard Campbell, *Human Ecology;* Harm J. de Blij and Peter O. Muller, *Geography: Regions and Concepts;* Erik P. Eckholm, *Losing Ground: Environmental Stress and World Food Prospects;* Arthur Getis, Judith Getis, and Jerome Fellmann, *Human Geography;* Andrew Goudie, *The Human Impact;* Joseph Bixby Hoyt, *Man and the Earth;* Jacquetta Hawkes, *The Atlas of Early Man;* Terry G. Jordan and Lester Rowntree, *The Human Mosaic;* Emilio F. Moran, *Human Adaptability;* Norman Myers, ed., *Gaia: An Atlas of Planet Management;* Charles Sheffield, *Man on Earth.*

Sources on the world's population include Lester R. Brown et al., *State of the World;* Population Reference Bureau, Inc., *World Population Data Sheet.*

Meet arid-land cultures in L. Berkofsky, D. Faiman, and J. Gale, *Settling the Desert;* J. L. Cloudsley-Thompson, *Man and the Biology of Arid Zones;* Uwe George, *In the Deserts of this Earth;* R. L. Heathcote, *The Arid Lands: Their Use and Abuse;* Dov Nir, *The Semi-Arid World;* Jake Page, *Arid Lands;* M. P. Petrov, *Deserts of the World.*

For more on arctic life see Franz Boas, *The Central Eskimo;* Roberto Bosi, *The Lapps;* Fred Bruemmer, *The Arctic World;* Sam Hall, *The Fourth World;* Jack Ives and Roger Barry, eds., *Arctic and Alpine Environments;* Martina Jacobs and James Richardson, eds., *Arctic Life;* Jean Malaurie, *The Last Kings of Thule;* Robert McGhee, *Canadian Prehistory;* Richard Nelson, *Hunters of the Northern Ice;* David Sugden, *Arctic and Antarctic.*

Books on islanders include Harold Brookfield, ed., *The Pacific in Transition;* Donald Fryer and James Jackson, *Indonesia;* Nigel Heseltine, *Madagascar;* David Lewis, *The Voyaging Stars;* Marion Steinmann, *Island Life;* John Terrell, *Prehistory in the Pacific Islands;* Richard F. Tomasson, *Iceland.*

Accounts of forest peoples can be found in Catherine Caufield, *In the Rainforest;* Napoleon A. Chagnon, *Yanomamö: The Fierce People;* Andrew W. Mitchell, *The Enchanted Canopy;* Emilio F. Moran, *Developing the Amazon;* Norman Myers, *The Primary Source: Tropical Forests and Our Future;* Colin M. Turnbull, *The Forest People.*

For more on grasslanders see Carol Beckwith and Tepilit Saitoti, *Maasai;* D. B. Grigg, *The Agricultural Systems of the World;* John Madson, *Where the Sky Began: Land of the Tallgrass Prairie;* Leslie Symons, *The Soviet Union;* Time-Life Books, *Grasslands and Tundra;* Donald Worster, *Dust Bowl.*

Books about highland cultures include Paul T. Baker, *The Biology of High-Altitude Peoples;* Paul T. Baker and Michael A. Little, *Man in the Andes;* Paula Brown, *Highland Peoples of New Guinea;* Paul and Elaine Lewis, *Peoples of the Golden Triangle;* Larry W. Price, *Mountains and Man;* Michael Tobias, ed., *Mountain People.*

Helpful references about people living near rivers include Richard Bangs and Christian Kallen, *Rivergods: Exploring the World's Great Wild Rivers;* Dennison Berwick, *A Walk Along the Ganges;* Russell Braddon et al., *River Journeys;* Richard Critchfield, *Shahhat: An Egyptian* and *Villages;* Alexander Frater, ed., *Great Rivers of the World;* Rand McNally's *Encyclopedia of World Rivers;* Henry David Thoreau, *A Week on the Concord and Merrimack Rivers;* Mark Twain, *Mississippi Writings.*

Books on coastal cultures include A. A. Abbie, *The Original Australians;* Victor Alba, *Peru;* Robert Edwards and Bruce Guerin, *Arnhem Land in Colour;* Jill Hunt, *Shanghai;* Wallace Kaufman and Orrin Pilkey, *The Beaches Are Moving: The Drowning of America's Shoreline;* Wesley Marx, *The Oceans, Our Last Resource;* Charles B. McLane, *Islands of the Mid-Maine Coast: Penobscot and Blue Hill Bays;* Max Schuchart, *The Netherlands.*

We also consulted many periodicals, including *Cultural Survival Quarterly,* UNESCO's *The Courier,* The American Geographical Society's *Focus, The Geographical Magazine,* and NATIONAL GEOGRAPHIC.

In addition, readers may consult the *National Geographic Index* and publication lists for a wealth of interesting works on human cultures worldwide.

ACKNOWLEDGMENTS

Our thanks to the many people and organizations who generously helped in the preparation of *Living on the Earth.* Special thanks go to James A. Hilliard and Kathy A. Kinney of R. R. Donnelley & Sons Co., Cartographic Services. We are also indebted to Robert Converse Bailey, U.C.L.A.; Ovid Bay, U. S. Department of Agriculture; Stephen A. Birdsall, Agricultural Commissioner's Office, Imperial County, CA; Robert A. Bisson, B.C.I. Geonetics, Inc.; Ernest S. "Tiger" Burch, Jr.; Bettie Calvery, Mobil; Paul Comar, National Marine Fisheries Service; John M. Crowley, University of Montana; Stephen L. Davis, Resource Managers Pty. Ltd., Australia; Gillian Feeley-Harnik, Johns Hopkins University; James Heitzman, Library of Congress; Patricia Jacobberger, Smithsonian Institution; Gerald J. Karaska, Clark University; Vivek Katju, Embassy of India; A. W. Küchler, University of Kansas; Philip Laun, Mobil; Thomas R. Leinbach, University of Kentucky; Peirce F. Lewis, Pennsylvania State University; Jacques Lombard, ORSTOM, Paris; John A. Macgregor, World Bank; Mervyn Meggitt, City University of New York; National Geographic Society's Judith F. Bell, Barry Bishop, Harm J. de Blij, and Suzanne Dupré, and the NGS Administrative Services, Library, Illustrations Library, Photographic Services, Records Library, Translations Division, Travel Office; Knut Schmidt-Nielsen, Duke University; Don Sillers, U. S. Agency for International Development; Nigel J. H. Smith, University of Florida; Wayne C. Starnes, Smithsonian Institution; Francis Tuan, U. S. Department of Agriculture; Christopher Uhl, Pennsylvania State University; Kathryn Zeimetz, U. S. Department of Agriculture.

We gratefully acknowledge permission to reprint excerpts from *Mountain People,* edited by Michael Tobias, © 1986 by the University of Oklahoma Press, as well as permission to use selected information from *Philips' Modern School Economic Atlas,* edited by Harold Fullard, © 1983 by George Philip & Son Ltd., and from *Biology of Plants* by Peter H. Raven, Ray F. Evert, and Susan E. Eichhorn, © 1986 by Worth Publishers, Inc.

AUTHORS

FRED BRUEMMER has been studying and photographing the Arctic for more than 30 years. He is the author and photographer of several books, including *The Arctic, Seasons of the Eskimo,* and *Arctic Animals.*

FAROUK EL-BAZ, Director of the Center for Remote Sensing at Boston University, is a native of Egypt and former science advisor to the late Egyptian President Anwar Sadat. He was a contributor to the National Geographic book, *The Desert Realm.*

DAVID LEWIS, physician-turned-mariner, has sailed around the world and visited many of its islands. He is the author of six NATIONAL GEOGRAPHIC articles and ten books, including *We, the Navigators* and *The Voyaging Stars.*

JOHN MADSON is noted for his works on nature and the outdoors. He has written three articles for NATIONAL GEOGRAPHIC and several books, including *Where the Sky Began, Stories From Under the Sky, Up On the River,* and *Out Home.*

MARVIN W. MIKESELL is Professor of Geography at the University of Chicago and past president of the Association of American Geographers. He is the author of *Northern Morocco: A Cultural Geography* and editor of *Geographers Abroad.*

BERNARD NIETSCHMANN is Professor of Geography at the University of California, Berkeley. He is the author of *Turtle Reef, Between Land and Water,* and *Caribbean Edge,* and was a contributor to the National Geographic book, *Lost Empires, Living Tribes.*

LARRY W. PRICE is Professor of Geography at Portland State University in Portland, Oregon. His many publications include the book, *Mountains and Man.*

MARGARET SEDEEN is a National Geographic writer and book editor. She has covered topics ranging through biography, science, social history, and geography, and was recently chief editor of the National Geographic book, *Great Rivers of the World.*

COLIN M. TURNBULL is Visiting Professor of Anthropology at Vassar College. He is the author of *The Human Cycle, The Forest People,* and other books on forest cultures.

INDEX

317

319

Type composition by the Typographic section of National Geographic Production Services, Pre-Press Division. Color separations by Chanticleer Co., Inc., New York, N.Y.; The Lanman Companies, Washington, D. C.; Lincoln Graphics Inc., Cherry Hill, N.J. Maps by R. R. Donnelley and Sons Co., Cartographic Services, Lancaster, Pa. Printed and bound by R. R. Donnelley and Sons Co., Chicago, Ill. Paper by Mead Paper Co., New York, N.Y.

Library of Congress CIP Data

Living on the earth.

Bibliography: p.
Includes index.
1. Human ecology. 2. Anthropo-geography.
I. National Geographic Society (U. S.)
GF41.L58 1988 304.2 88-1440
ISBN 0-87044-734-3
ISBN 0-87044-735-1 (deluxe)
ISBN 0-87044-736-X (lib. bdg.)

You are invited to join the National Geographic Society or to send gift memberships to others. (Membership includes a subscription to the NATIONAL GEOGRAPHIC magazine.) For information call 1-800-638-4077 toll free, or write to the National Geographic Society, Washington, D. C. 20036.